LIPSTICK
FOOTBALL

Praise for LIPSTICK FOOTBALL

"With a bold, ferocious tone, this book dares the reader to go after dreams with the grit, resilience and smarts of a championship team."

"Your whole section on Leaping really spoke to me! When I had already "decided" to not take action that day, I said, "Put down the book and go do it!" And I did!"

"While Lipstick Football does deliver some interesting insights to the game, it also has a larger purpose of taking lessons from football and using them as a framework for motivational thinking."

"I LOVE the 40-second timer to put my play in motion! I've used that technique every day since the first day I read about it, and it works. It's been a game changer for me!"

"Weynand's conversational, down-to-earth voice coaches her readers to reflect, regroup and charge ahead even in life's most challenging moments."

"I love the idea of getting a real football as a touchstone!"

"With its extended metaphor of football and life, Lipstick Football makes visual the often-vague process of achieving dreams."

"Weynand's mantra is not just carpe diem – seize the day. It's carpe vita – seize life!"

"Whether it's explaining cognitive disfluency or interacting with hummingbirds, the author takes Xs and Os to a whole new level. She not only shares her comprehensive knowledge of football but demonstrates in easy-to-follow fashion how to use game concepts to unlock the potential every person already has."

"Five stars. Excellent insights in getting people to take action."

"This book is a great read."

LIPSTICK
FOOTBALL

8 GAME-CHANGING PRINCIPLES

TO BUST THROUGH LIMITATIONS AND ACHIEVE THE IMPOSSIBLE
WHILE LEARNING THE GAME OF FOOTBALL

DIANA WEYNAND

LIPSTICK FOOTBALL
8 Game-Changing Principles to Break Through Limitations and Achieve the
Impossible While Learning the Game of Football

By Diana Weynand

Published by Second Side Press
secondsidepress@gmail.com

The following trademarks are owned by 2nd Side Adventures, LLC:
Lipstick Football™
Mastermind Your Life™

Cover design by Sam Arts Studio
Back cover photo by Diana Lundin
Illustrations by Diana Weynand
Image permissions in the Acknowledgements

ISBN: 978-1-884029-01-1 (paperback color)
ASIN: B09BBQGF5S (eBook)

Visit the Author's Websites:
www.LipstickFootball.com
www.MastermindLife.com

Dedication

Good things come in threes.

To all the women in this book
who didn't take "No" for an answer.

For my mother, Dee Weynand—
an avid football fan and ferocious lover of life.
Although she'll never hold this book in her hands,
her early support of my dream to write it
helped make it a reality.

And for my friend Bobbi Kennedy—
I will be forever blessed by your friendship
and your 10,000-foot view of life and the great beyond.

Join the LIPSTICK FOOTBALL League!

Subscribe to the LIPSTICK Football League and download your FREE exercise from Diana Weynand's upcoming book, *LIPSTICK FOOTBALL Workbook* (coming Fall 2021). The exercise will help bring into focus your "Action Evolution," which Weynand introduces in chapter 9 of this book.

www.LipstickFootball.com/action

Throughout this book, there are references to videos and articles that provide a deeper dive into the LIPSTICK Football Method. You can find those "extras" at:

www.LipstickFootball.com/extras

For all other inquiries, contact:

info@LipstickFootball.com

Acknowledgements

My deepest gratitude for those who kept me on the playing field and focused on the end zone. To separate species, I'll start with my dog, Sadie. Thanks for your patience, sweet girl. A big cookie is coming your way.

Special thanks to my offensive line: Shirley Craig, Judith Branzburg, Catherine Kerr, Pam Hughes, Lynne Weynand and Tina Valinsky.

To my secondary defense for dotting Is, crossing Ts, occasional arm-chair sports commentary and ongoing support: Marina Aris, Marilyn Buckner, Sean P. Carlin, John Cartwright, Melinda Coss, Phil Deustch, Vivian Deustch, Gundi Gabrielle, Peggy Glenn, Shirl Hendryx, Esther Hicks, Steve Hochman, Sylvia Holland, Carole A. Oglesby, Ellen Rozman, George Weynand, Sam Weynand, Justine Willis and Kathleen Young.

To the coaches who provided invaluable input on plays and strategies: Tim DeRuyter, Defensive Coach of the Oregon Ducks (Eugene, OR) and Jason Sabolic, Head Football Coach at El Camino Real Charter High School (Los Angeles, CA).

To special team members: Anne Fletcher who enlightened me on how to immerse, and to my first and forever Mastermind Your Life team who embraced my out-of-the-box approach to life coaching and motivation.

To the women in football who encouraged and welcomed my LIPSTICK Football method: Lisa King (Commissioner of the Women's Football Alliance), Odessa Jenkins (Co-Founder of the Women's National Football Conference) and Johanna Wood (President of New Zealand Football).

To the following individuals, companies and organizations who granted permission to use their images in this book:

National Football League logos provided through the courtesy of the NFL: Aries Tabligue, Senior Coordinator, Trademark and Brand Protection.

LA Rams uniform and helmet images provided through the courtesy of the Los Angeles Rams: Cory Befort (Senior Director, Creative Services), Chase Isaacs (Manager, Corporate Communications) and Melissa Park (Specialist, Marketing and Media Operations).

Virtual lines field image provided through the courtesy of SportsMEDIA Technology (SMT): Patricia G. Hopkins, Corporate Vice President, Marketing.

Scoreboard and play clock images provided through the courtesy of All American Scoreboards: Tom Ellington, National Account Director.

Shoulder pad images provided through the courtesy of Douglas Pads and Sports, Inc.: Ryan Huntsman, Vice President & COO.

Cramer integrated padded pants image provided through the courtesy of Performance Health: Dave Caruthers, Director of Operations.

Football chain set image provided through the courtesy of Rogers Athletic Company: Ryan Collier, Advertising Director.

Sarah Fuller image and tweet provided through the courtesy of Vanderbilt Athletics: Sarah Fetters, Director of Football Communications.

NFL and NCAA football images provided through the courtesy of Wilson Sporting Goods.

Contents

Chapter 9 ➤ KICK 151

Chapter 10 ➤ LEARNING TO WIN 175

Preface

I never imagined I would write a book about football and life. Yes, there was a time I wanted to apply my football experience and hands-on training skills to break down the game into digestible bits, to create a football primer "for the rest of us." And there was a time I wanted to write a motivational book, a sort of bootcamp for life, based on my Mastermind Your Life™ trainings.

Before I completed either one, an extraordinary thing happened—they collided in my mind. I couldn't watch a football game without getting a "kick" of motivation for a current project. I couldn't work on a project without thinking of a specific aspect of football. I was living a mashup. It was fun—and I loved it! The more I leaned into what the sport of football could teach me about life, the more inspired I became.

This book is an invitation to learn about football—not as the "all-American sport" it is, but as a way of taking charge of your life, of giving your dreams structure and helping you get downfield to score in *your* end zone.

Utilizing the LIPSTICK Football principles feels magical to me. I'd like to share that magic with you.

Diana Weynand
Los Angeles, CA, July 2021

I eat "No" for breakfast.

—Kamala Harris
Vice President of the United States

Chapter 1

LIPSTICK FOOTBALL LEAGUE

Want to learn about football? Maybe pick up some terminology? Watch a game with friends or family and really enjoy it? Understand the rules? Follow key players? Keep up with the action? Maybe even anticipate the action?

If you said yes to any of these questions, then you'll find what you need in this book—plenty of football to get your head in the game.

But wait, there's more...

What if you made it personal?

What if, in learning about football, you also learned the eight principles that make the game exciting, that make teams click and make players shine? What if these principles could make a difference in your life—help guide your long-term plans and your short-term plays? What if they could give you a leg up on achieving your personal goals, growth and desires? What if they could make you shine?

For as long as I can remember, watching football has inspired me—to try harder, face a challenge, pick a different approach, build a better team, play like a quarterback, think like a coach, and never give up. You name it. I get everything I need to inspire my life journey—through football.

I'm confident I can teach you the game of football, and I'll tell you why in this chapter. But I also want to teach you how to grab life by the collar and say, "Hey you, come with me." That's really what I want to talk about in these pages. Not just *carpe diem*—seize the day. I want to teach you to *carpe vita*—seize life.

So here's the deal. In this book, I will provide a safe space for you to learn football and build your confidence around the game. Now will you take a leap with me? Will you get to know the eight LIPSTICK Football principles and apply them to your own life? Will you use them as a guide to put your body in motion and claim those extra yards on your own field of dreams? And will you do it with the ferocity of a professional football player?

If you said yes—Atta girl!

You belong in the LIPSTICK Football League.

Football DNA

I'm a problem solver. When I stepped into a Las Vegas elevator and saw a man wearing a Green Bay Packers baseball hat, I was thrilled. It was Super Bowl weekend, 2008. I'd recently watched a playoff game with the Packers and was left with a nagging question. In the third quarter of the game, Green Bay's defense seemed to come unglued and they lost the game. Why did that happen?

I pointed to the man's hat, smiled and asked, "So what happened to Green Bay's defense in the third quarter?" Simple, direct question. He said, "The defensive coach failed to adjust." Simple, direct answer. But not enough to really satisfy my curiosity. I replied, "What do you mean--he called the wrong plays?" With a slight frustration, the man repeated, "He failed to adjust. He simply failed to adjust." An awkward silence arose.

I knew I was smart enough to understand, but no real explanation was given. Another man entered the elevator and the two started talking easily about the game, which made my frustration grow. The man I spoke to hadn't missed a Green

Bay game in 30 years. Remarkable. Yet he couldn't break down that one phrase any further—at least, not to my liking. Why did it have to be so mysterious? Why couldn't our conversation continue?

In that moment, my interest in Green Bay's defense receded and I started forming a different question. Why couldn't that elevator chap, clearly a lifelong football fan, answer my very simple question? Was it because I'm a woman and he's a man? Was it a Venus vs Mars thing? That seemed way too simple an answer. No, I decided. It's about football experience and DNA. Men have it—women don't.

Most men get to know football through hands-on experience—from a dad who teaches them to throw a spiral the moment their tiny hands can hold a ball. Or by playing football in school. By the time they reach adulthood, men often see the game through experienced eyes where rules, plays and strategies form an intricate web of possibilities, sort of like 3D chess. When they step out of that web, into 2D checkers, they can get stuck explaining the game to anyone who missed that DNA-like experience growing up.

Most women weren't handed a football when they were young or taught to throw a spiral. I was lucky. I grew up playing street football with a big brother and flag football in a neighborhood lot, and I eventually played women's tackle football. I know what it's like to suit up in protective football gear and physically block another player from crossing an imaginary line. I wish all women could benefit from that experience. It was life-changing for me.

And so was that interaction in the Las Vegas elevator with the Green Bay fan. That's when I decided to start a conversation about football—for the rest of us. As author, I promise to keep things simple as I lay a foundation of the game, the players, positions, strategies and rules. I'll speak in a language that's friendly to folks who don't already know the game. And maybe, together, we can create a new, smart and savvy strand of football DNA.

Women's Professional Football

I'll never forget that sunny Saturday morning in the summer of 2001. The Los Angeles Lasers were holding tryouts for their first season in the western division of the WPFL—the Women's Professional Football League. Wait, what? Women's professional tackle football? Yes.

I, along with about 60 other women on the field, were living our dream. We were part of history—and we knew it. It was empowering and fun! And while you didn't see it, you could hear that glass ceiling crack and shatter as we kicked, ran and threw footballs from one side of the field to the other. In chapter 9, you will learn more about women in football today—from high school sports to professional leagues, including the NFL.

While there were big hearts on our team, including mine, and a lot of talent, the coaches weren't prepared to motivate or develop women's skills in football. It was new. Remember, most guys at that time had football DNA—most women didn't. The training and terminology weren't always effective or clear. After a few weeks of mismanaged practices and trying to tackle women who towered six inches above me or outweighed me by 35 pounds, I got injured and had to step off the field.

I thought I could make a difference for these women, so I stayed on and took the role of general manager—supporting the team members, scheduling practices and organizing our season of games. Once my stitches healed, I got into uniform and back out on the field as defensive end, a position that made me shine (I'll tell you why in chapter 5).

I was part of something extraordinary—the emergence of women's professional football—and I wear my Harry Potter-like cleat scar as a badge of honor. I also learned some valuable life lessons during those WPFL days. The main one is this: in football and in life, you've got to put yourself on the field if you want to play the game.

Me in the role of general manager for the Los Angeles Lasers

I'm creating a new field and space where football meets life, where knowledge from one can be used to frame the other. Where glass ceilings can be shattered and new opportunities revealed. What seemed impossible—women taking on roles in professional football—is finally starting to become the norm. Although the lines of possibility may be a little blurry, I promise they'll become clearer as you start your journey and step onto the field.

Cracking a Marble

The position of general manager of the LA Lasers was a good fit. I love to empower and inspire, and, in my heart, I am—have been and probably always will be—a teacher and coach. One of my favorite quotes is from the philosopher Maimonides (I took some liberty with the pronouns): "Give a woman a fish and you feed her for a day; teach a woman to fish and you feed her for a lifetime."

My drive to teach and empower led to a career in the film and television industry as the co-owner of a media technology training business. My company's specialty is developing boot-camp style training for artists—film and video editors, colorists, graphic artists and others—on how to operate complex software and equipment used in the production of films and television shows.

By crafting courses using real-world scenarios, I teach operators skills they need to perform specific tasks quickly and efficiently. Over the years, I've written 15+ "how-to" books using a step-by-step approach to tackling creative challenges. In addition to film and television training, I've taught dynamic visualization—a technique athletes and others use to mentally rehearse successful outcomes. And over the years, I've used my degrees in music education to teach songwriting, piano and voice lessons.

No matter the topic, my signature training approach is to break down any goal into achievable action steps. I like to think of it as cracking a marble, which I loved to do as a child. On the outside, a round glass cracked marble feels hard and impenetrable. But peek inside, and the fracture lines look like tiny roads or paths leading to a destination. Any goal or journey in life can feel impenetrable like a glass marble. The trick is to crack that marble, then trace the pathways to your goal.

As your coach on this journey, I'm going to make a bold promise. Watching football, or playing it, and applying the LIPSTICK Football Principles can help you crack your own impenetrable marble and live your best life as you trek forward in the direction of your dreams.

The LIPSTICK Football Principles

We all subscribe to certain life principles—whether or not we take the time to carve them out for ourselves, borrow them from society, or passively accept those handed down to us by previous generations.

For me, on any given fall Sunday over the years, I saw principles I wanted to live by—right there on the football field. I saw players leap into action, immerse themselves in the moment, shine when they performed their personal best. I saw a level of commitment and dedication that was contagious—that I wanted to bring to my own life.

Through watching, playing and studying the game, I've identified eight principles that represent fundamental truths and provide a code of conduct for playing football and living life. Did someone hand me these principles? No. I had to grasp them for myself, as anyone does when she takes the step of defining what's important to her. And as a coach and teacher, I wanted to share them to empower others.

To make my set of principles easy to remember, I decided to use an acronym. And because I wanted to leave a red mark on the football glass ceiling, I chose LIPSTICK.

Here are my LIPSTICK Football principles.

	PRINICPLE
L	Leap
I	Immerse
P	Play
S	Shine
T	Track
I	Initiate
C	Condition
K	Kick

What do you gain from following a clear set of principles? Psychologists say... a lot! Principles identify priorities and beliefs. They're like road signs that guide your choices and actions as you move toward your destination—whether that's in a work environment, on a personal project or on a football field.

As you make choices that align with a principle, you spend less time worrying about whether or not you're doing the right thing. You enjoy more confidence and peace of mind—and have a better chance of feeling fulfilled. Unless you take the time to define or acknowledge your principles, they can't do their job of guiding you effectively.

The LIPSTICK Football principles guide my personal choices and actions. They motivate me, lift me up and inspire me. They remind me to focus on what's important as I keep moving forward. I believe the LIPSTICK Football principles can give you the support you need to score on your own playing field.

Football Topics

Let's crack the marble and break down the LIPSTICK Football principles even further by assigning a single aspect of football to each principle. Leaning into the underlying principle of a football topic will give you a broader perspective, and perhaps a better grasp, of what's important about that part of the game.

Here are the LIPSTICK Football principles aligned with eight specific football topics:

	PRINICPLE	FOOTBALL TOPIC
L	Leap	Taking Sides
I	Immerse	Suiting Up
P	Play	Hitting the Field
S	Shine	Getting into Position
T	Track	Rules of the Game
I	Initiate	Making Plays
C	Condition	Building Routines
K	Kick	Women in Football

There's a progressive order to both the principles and football topics. For example, you have to know the field layout before you know where players line up. And you have to take a leap in life before you know where you shine. Since the LIPSTICK Football principles and football topics follow a specific order, I recommend starting at the beginning and going through to the end. Once you're familiar with the principles, refer to them whenever you need them.

Watching or experiencing football through the lens of these eight principles has taken the game to another level for me. I no longer just tune in and look at the scoreboard. I watch life unfold as human effort. And that's pretty exciting stuff.

Applying the Principles

In his book *Smarter Faster Better: The Transformative Power of Real Productivity,* Charles Duhigg shares studies on cognitive *disfluency.* These studies prove the more we engage our brain while we're learning something, the better we'll be able to process, encode and retrieve the information. In non-scientific terms, it simply means that the more you *do* while learning, the better you'll learn and even remember. Cognitive disfluency is a good thing.

People who take notes by hand? They'll have better and quicker access to the material than those who typed notes on a computer, which is an automatic, non-thinking activity. To write by hand engages the brain in a much different way. If you draw a colorful picture to clarify a lecture or webinar, all the better. That information could last even longer and have a deeper imprint. You might even reduce stress and have fun in the process.

The reverse is cognitive *fluency*—processing information with ease. When doing something seems easy, or when thinking about something feels fluid, your brain probably isn't working very hard. Sometimes that's exactly what you want—a mindless diversion. Watching sports can give you that, for sure. But when you want to learn something, remember it and retrieve it later, going out of your way to disrupt your learning process has proven to be a more effective approach.

You could read this book and gain a lot of knowledge. That would be cognitive fluency. Read and absorb. But I want you to get a *feel* for football—as well as life through the lens of the LIPSTICK Football principles. That's harder. To do that, you need to read, absorb and *do.* You need to put yourself into action and use your senses to deepen your connection with the game and your life. At the end of each chapter, you'll find a "Break It Down" section to help you do just that.

Don't be shy. If you purchased this book, it's because you wanted to learn something new, which you will—so dive in. But don't miss the opportunity to *try* something new. As you read and learn, I encourage you to take an active role in the learning process. Go ahead—shoot for a 10 on the cognitive disfluency scale. You'll be glad you did. And if you would like to journal your thoughts or keep track of your progress, you can do that in the *LIPSTICK FOOTBALL Journal: From Leap to Kick* (available at www.LipstickFootball.com/extras).

The Game Plan

Every good coach has a game plan. Here's mine. I'll kick off each chapter with a principle followed by a specific football topic. One chapter, one principle, one football focus. I recommend the immersion approach. Read a chapter, consider the principle and study the football topic associated with that principle. When you're comfortable with that principle and topic, move on to the following chapter.

Next, watch a game and look for the key aspects outlined in the chapter. If you need some guidance, follow the steps provided in the "Break It Down" section at the end of each chapter. In the Fall, you can tune into a live televised game—either high school, college or professional—every day of the week, except Tuesday and Wednesday. If you can't attend an NFL game, find out which high schools or colleges play football locally. You can watch recorded games on a variety of sports channels and online sites, including YouTube.

Along the way, I'll encourage you to practice what you can. Is it decent weather for pacing out a local football field? What about buying a football that fits your hand? Some things you'll have to imagine, like how a football player suits up. There are two distinct sides to a football team and you'll learn the specific positions on each side. This is where those famous Xs and Os come in. There are lots of rules in football, but I won't bury you with them. I'll focus on the basics and introduce you to the officials who maintain order on the field.

If you allow the LIPSTICK Football principles to guide you and use the game of football as a sort of template for your journey, I believe you will feel motivated and inspired to carpe vita—seize life. If football is new territory for you, I've got you covered. As you know, I've played professional football (I love saying that). More importantly, one of my life principles is to share knowledge and empower people, especially if they don't have a lot of football DNA.

Whew! Lots to do. Are you ready to dive in *and* have some fun? If so, welcome to the LIPSTICK Football League. There's room here for everyone.

Now—let's hit it!

Huddle Up

"Huddle up" is a term you'll hear around football—both on the field and off. When players and coaches say it, it means to gather in a tight circle because someone has something important to say. Maybe the coach has a new strategy to try, or a player wants to motivate the team or share a personal insight. During a game, the team huddles together to get their marching orders for the next play. After the game, the team huddles up to celebrate or to chant "We're number one!"

Throughout this book, I'll end each chapter with a Huddle Up section to reinforce your new football knowledge with a LIPSTICK Football principle.

Dallas Cowboys huddle around quarterback Tony Romo (#9)

Break It Down

Just as football teams huddle up to recap, they also invest time finessing their skills. But first, they have to "break it down"— observe and identify specific actions that will help improve what or how they're doing something.

I invite you to use each "Break It Down" section throughout this book to go beyond just learning about football. I invite you to have fun, get involved in the game, and see how each LIPSTICK Football principle is at play on the field and in your own life.

FOOTBALL

1. Where is the closest football field in your neighborhood? Who plays there, and when?

2. Schedule a time when you can go and watch a game. Maybe take a friend that doesn't know football so you can teach them what you've learned.

3. Did your college have a football team? Look up when its games are televised and watch. If you have a favorite NFL team—great! If not, find the closest NFL team to where you live and follow them. You can find an NFL Teams Map on my website (www.LipstickFootball.com/extras).

LIFE

1. Some things in life need unpacking—some don't. Take a minute to consider your connection to the game. Do you enjoy watching football today? If yes, why? If not, why not? Maybe you have fond memories of watching the game with your family, friend, or mate. Or throwing a football with friends on the beach.

2. We often take principles for granted. Remember, a principle is a fundamental truth, rule or code of conduct created to frame priorities and guide you toward desired actions. Write down any principles you currently hold and practice.

3. To exercise cognitive disfluency, don't forget to add hands-on experience to what you're learning. If you like the "Crack the Marble" concept, watch the how-to video on my website (www.LipstickFootball.com/extras) and have fun cracking your own marbles.

Chapter 2

LEAP

Taking Sides

The hardest thing to listen to—your instincts, your human personal intuition—always whispers. It never shouts. So, you have to, every day of your lives, be ready to hear what whispers in your ear. If you can listen to the whisper, and if it tickles your heart, then... we will benefit from everything you do.

—Steven Spielberg, American Filmmaker

Imagine this. You're a diver at a swim meet, poised on the edge of the platform. You're still, motionless, calm—visualizing what will unfold in the next moment. In an instant, you dive from the edge into the pool below. Or you're at the starting line of a race, in "set" position—knees bent, one foot forward, fingers and hands spread out for support. You wait—still, motionless, calm. The race gun fires, and you spring into full sprint toward the finish line. Or you're on a football field. Two teams line up facing each other. Each waits to explode into action with a clear focus on their goal. Blue—42—Hike!

Leaping into action is bold. It's definitive. Powerful. It has to be. A leap puts your intentions into motion signaling you've found something you really want. Something that requires more than observing from a distance. Something that requires stepping out on the platform or up to the line and putting your life into action, or action into your life. When you leap, you send a Tarzan-like cry to the Universe, "I'm coming, ahh-ahh-ahh." Leaping is a bold act of communication—both external and internal—to the world and to yourself.

Introducing the L Principle — LEAP

Leaping is often thought of as the singular act of jumping off, moving forward or taking action toward a goal. But leaping is really two things. It's jumping off, for sure. There's no leaping if there's no action towards something. Yet the moment of calm before the leap is equally powerful. That moment may not be long, yet it has the potential to redirect you. It's the necessary prelude to *right* action—an action that will yield a positive or productive result.

In a football game, if front-line offensive players don't hold steady before the start of a play—if a player shifts from their "set" position, moves or even twitches—that player's team is given a "false start" penalty. It's no different in life. If you jump the gun and act without thought or intention, without looking for the right action, you can be penalized, too, by veering off course and onto a less expedient path to your goal.

You'll always see the external expression of your leap, as will anyone watching you. But it's important to ask yourself what brought you to the edge of action. Did you hear an inner voice whisper a thought—maybe something creative to do or achieve? Something to learn or become? Was there a hint of a new dream that could take flight? These hints are special gifts. Don't toss them aside as irrelevant or assume they would come to anyone else in that moment. If *you* heard it, the message was personal and most definitely meant for you.

Your intuition, your inner voice, is where the seeds of your dream lie. Your job is to listen for the internal cues and follow their lead. The great filmmaker, Steven Spielberg, who has created some of the most impactful films ever produced, acknowledges the power of the pre-leap moment in the words that open this chapter. If you don't listen for the gentle knocks at your heart's door, you might miss out on opportunities to leap into action and align with your dream. And the world would miss out on you and your gifts.

Once you do take a leap of action, expect it to throw into play other actions, or reactions, that will stimulate both positive *and* negative forces. And one of two things will happen—you will either fall or fly. When you leap and fall, it's usually because obstacles emerge, STOP signs show up out of nowhere. Old personal programming you thought was long resolved taunts you. "You can't do this." "What are you thinking?" "Who do you think you are?" These stumbling blocks can derail the most bravehearted.

When you leap and fly, you soar and feel the wind beneath your wings. Your energies align, as though an "Open" sign is hanging on your heart's front door.

There is a trick to flying more and falling less. Anticipate that your action, no matter how small, might just be powerful enough to cause a reaction. If you stand tall and call out the reaction for what it is—a pesky obstacle—the Universe will get a pretty good idea of how much heart you have for realizing your dream. And it will back you up 100%.

Do you have the heart to take a leap? Every goal, endeavor or person worth investing in requires a leap. Call it a leap of faith, if you want. Whether it's braving the vulnerabilities of a new relationship, going after a potential job opportunity, or trying your hand at a creative endeavor, you must take action to get what you want. What you will find when you leap is that you will both fall and fly. That's how you learn and grow. You listen, then leap.

You fall, then fly—higher and higher—getting closer and closer to your desire.

The dynamics of a football team, which I cover in this chapter, will be easy to grasp. Yet "Leap" might be the most complex of the eight principles because it's about aligning that very important first step of the journey with your destination. Sally Ride, the first American woman in space, said, "All adventures, especially into new territory, are scary."

Since you're heading into new territory, take some time to reflect on your own dynamics. And as you leap into learning about football, find ways you can leap into action in your own life.

Two Sides and a Ball

The first thing I learned playing street football is that it only takes a few players to have fun and score. That's true with a lot of team sports—football, soccer, basketball. Wherever folks gather—street, park, field, or school—players pick sides, grab a ball and start playing. Two sides and a ball. One side has possession of the ball and tries to score with it. The other side tries to stop forward progress.

It turns out, that's all that's needed to play a football game in an 80,000-person stadium—two sides and a ball. The factors and organization involved in professional football make it a lot more complex, of course. Rather than a few scruffy individuals, the players on an NFL field are two highly organized teams, and each team has two sides. One side takes the field *with* the ball and tries to score, while the other side takes the field to stop the opponent from advancing the ball. At any given moment during a game, a player has a singular intent and focus on one side or the other. Two sides and a ball.

The two sides of football action are a perfect example of the Leap principle. When you leap, you put two dynamics into play—an action creates a reaction. In football, those two dynamics cycle between initiating forward motion and blocking forward motion.

In a single game there will be dozens of these cycles. Turns out, the dynamic exchange of energy flow is as much a part of football as it is of life.

Offense and Possession

In football, the more frequently a team gets possession of the ball, the more opportunities it has to score. There are football statistics, or "stats," that reflect "time of possession" throughout a game and for the season.

The group of players who have possession of the ball is the offense. The offense initiates actions that move the ball down the field in a variety of ways—by running, throwing or kicking it. You will learn more about football plays in chapter 7. For now, know that the job of the offense is singularly focused—to move the ball down the field and score.

If you look at life as a football game, you will see offensive players and moves all around you. Don't laugh—look around. Is everything always on an equal footing? Or is someone stepping in to take charge and initiate an action? It doesn't matter where. Could be in the office or in the kitchen. Someone is putting something into motion. Think of dating. Who makes the first offensive move or play? Which one of you initiates the first kiss? Who asks whom to marry?

These are offensive moves. It's not that the other person or team is passive. They might be working their tail off to field a play you initiated. I was once so thrown by someone saying an unexpected, "I love you," I had to sit down and take it in. Offensive plays can throw you. But in football, as in life, you don't always have time to sit down and think about it. When the game clock is ticking, you've got to act. And that's the offense—always leaping into action.

You Gotta Have Heart!

Let's face it. The moment the offense gets the ball, they're going to get roughed up, kicked around, knocked down. Players from the other team will try to steal the ball from them. The offense has to hold on tight—and not just to the ball. They have to hold on to how much they want to be in possession of the ball. They have to be unequivocal and determined, otherwise they'll lose focus and the other side will snatch the ball right out of their hands.

Simply put, what makes an offense great is heart. Miles and miles and miles of heart. The offense has to burn with desire. Otherwise, why the heck are they even on the playing field?

Let's translate that to your life. If you want something badly enough, you have to have the heart to go after it—to leap for it. But first, you have to listen to that inner voice to learn what might move you the most. What are you the most determined to have or achieve? What are you willing to risk the most for? Or turn it around. What would you fear or regret not accomplishing?

A few years after my mother died, I had mortality on my mind—that sense of a clock ticking in the background, a reminder that time was finite. I asked myself, "What would I regret not having completed should I die tomorrow?" A faint voice replied instantly. "I'd regret I didn't do more with my songwriting." Wow—what a clear and instantaneous message. I'd fallen in love with songwriting earlier in my life, yet chose a career path outside of music. With this gentle nudge, I started writing songs again, and have since placed my music on television shows as a secondary career.

It's never easy being on offense—picking up the ball and running with it. People want to steal it from you—steal the joy you have of carrying it. It turns out I'd left a piece of my heart, my own personal football, out on the field. I was yearning to pick it up and carry it forward, to move it downfield. I could have pointed to life's circumstances and found a ton of reasons to justify why I'd dropped the ball. None of those justifications would have moved me forward. The important thing is that—on hearing that faint whisper—I acknowledged how much I wanted to write songs again and I leaped into action.

Your desire doesn't have to be big or grand to be satisfying. But it will have a better chance of survival when you allow yourself to want it with all your heart.

Defense—an Equal and Opposite Force

Back in 1686, Isaac Newton presented his three observational laws of motion. The third law is analogous to football—and life. Basically, Newton observed that objects in play have a reaction to each other. For every action or force in nature, there is an equal and opposite reaction.

Remember that first kiss? That was an offensive action. What was the reaction? Kiss back? Turn away? If a football team's offense has heart and is willing to move heaven and earth to score, then leave it to their opponent's defense to try and shut down the offense with equal force.

Offense against defense for possession of the ball is what football is all about. Two sides—one ball. In the 1996 sports film *Jerry Maguire* starring Tom Cruise as Maguire, there is a scene at the end of the movie in which he humbly says to his love interest and business associate, "You complete me." That's what any defense does—it completes the cycle of action initiated by the offense. It doesn't know what play the offense is going to run, so it looks for clues or signs—a twitch here, a nod there, a shoulder dip, a head turn—and then reacts. Action—then reaction. Offense—then defense.

Isn't that what happens in life? The moment you put your mind toward what you want, some force—something or someone—comes in and shuts you down. Slams the door on your hopes and dreams. Doubts, delays, old habits, and ancient mental programs sneak into play. They throw you off balance. And the stronger your desire, the tougher the defense. In other words, once you initiate your offense and put your desire into action, your defense will kick in with some measure of force. Whoever pushes with the most force typically wins the battle.

Thanks to Mr. Newton, I no longer move forward blindly in pursuit of my goal, as though I might frolic in the daisies or tiptoe through the tulips along the way. I now operate with the knowledge that the moment I take a leap and lay down a convincing offense, I'll be met with an equally determined defense—usually of my own making. But knowing that, expecting that opposing force and not shying away from it, gives me an advantage on the playing field.

The Great Observer

Isaac Newton was minding his own business reading a book under an apple tree when a falling apple caught his eye (cartoonists like to show it hitting his head). He didn't just scratch his head, turn the page of his book and keep reading. He observed that action and gave deep and serious thought as to *why* and *how* that apple fell. He was later able to publish his law of universal gravity and the related three laws of motion.

Just as Newton observed the apple falling from the tree and embraced the role of a detached observer, someone has to observe and develop both offense and defense in order to build a winning football team.

Enter—the football coach.

The role of a football coach is to observe and evaluate offensive and defensive skills on the team. Of the potential 53 active players on an NFL team's roster, who's looking good in what position? Who should come off the bench or sit out the next play? The NFL allows only 46 players to suit up for a game. Which ones will the coach pick to play, and why?

Unlike street football, where you play whenever you can grab the time or people, organized football has a season. A football coach has a long-term goal for every season and makes strategic choices to support that goal. Is it to win the Super Bowl—the granddaddy of football championships? If that's out of reach for a team in the current season, a coach might choose a different goal: say, to strengthen the defense or improve the team's running game.

A coach has many roles—game strategy, team building, motivation. One of the primary roles is to balance the forces of offense and defense on the team. Sort of like how a third leg balances a three-legged stool.

A Three-Legged Stool

Picture this. You're watching a favorite TV show while sitting on a three-legged stool. Unfortunately, there's no remote control for the TV and no DVR to record what you're watching. Like life, the program will keep playing no matter what happens or who calls. As you're watching TV, sitting on the stool—a super-solid sitting device—one of the legs breaks. Was that leg weaker? Were you rocking on the stool or leaning too heavily on just one leg? It happens. Life requires constant finesse to stay in balance.

So, you've got a broken stool *and* you can't stop the show. What are you going to focus on now? The show or the stool?

When something in life breaks, no matter how small, it throws your focus and process off balance. When that happens, you usually stop focusing on what you want and instead key into what's broken. Focusing on what's broken can often become an obsession—one that happens to be very effective at keeping you from achieving your goals.

Taking a leap is the first LIPSTICK Football principle. Think of it as the "Offensive" leg of the stool. You make the first move by saying, "This is what I want." Once you leap toward your target, get ready to feel the "Defensive" leg start to wiggle and throw you off balance. That "wiggle" might appear as a personal obstacle, such as an old routine or bad habit. It could also be a worn-out belief or expectation.

The third leg is the disruptive force, and I don't mean a noisy child screaming to have its way. The third leg of the stool is the coach. The coach's job is to restore balance to the three-legged stool—i.e., your life—by balancing your own offensive and defensive forces.

When life starts to get messy, and you feel that defensive leg start to wiggle, lean into the third leg, your inner coach. It will keep you sitting straight and allow you to enjoy the journey.

Invite Perspective

Throughout this chapter, I've talked about action—then reaction. Where does the observant coach sit on your personal team? A coach is not a catalyst. The offense is the catalyst. The coach doesn't try to tackle anyone. The defense does that quite nicely, thank you. Why do you even need a coach?

Consider a film director. She has a preconceived idea of what she wants from an actor, an emotional point she hopes the actor will bring to the scene. From behind the camera, or off to the side, the director monitors the scene. Is she getting what she wants? Are the actors hitting their marks? Observe and direct.

This combination of observation and direction is a great scheme for a lot of things, including life. If I said, "You need a good coach," would you think I meant hiring someone to motivate you or help you accomplish your goals? What I'm really suggesting is that you become your *own* coach to observe and direct your actions. If taking on the persona of a good coach doesn't feel right, try director, teacher, conductor or personal advocate.

You might ask how you can see yourself from a coach's perspective when you're a player on the field. The key is distance—distance creates perspective. When coaches step off the field, they gain a point of view that allows them to analyze their players' actions. Film directors watch a scene from behind the cameras. Theater directors walk to the back of the theater to observe. Music producers listen from inside the sound booth.

Each perch or position creates the perspective needed to see the bigger picture and to know whether the forces at play are achieving the desired results.

After you leap and all hell breaks loose, take a step back and invite that perspective. Look for ways to balance your energetic forces. You will find that, with the wise counsel of your inner coach, you can clear a track for your offense and minimize resistance from your defense, which will speed up your results and help you stick to your path. You just need to get started—by taking that initial brave leap.

Huddle Up

As I mentioned earlier in this chapter, getting your head around football's offense and defense isn't such a big deal. Two sides and a ball. But understanding the dynamics between forces of nature can be. To hold a steady course, you balance those forces with an observing coach. But don't forget, you have to leap and put something into action before the fun can begin.

To review, the Leap Cycle consists of three steps:

1) Identify what you want and take action toward it.

2) Don't be blindsided. Expect to see or feel a reaction after you leap.

3) Observe and negotiate the two forces to ensure you stay on course and reach your goal.

As you develop skills in each of these areas—taking an offensive leap, side stepping a defense, and directing your progress like a good coach—you will become unstoppable. You will feel more confident and in control of your team. You will feel the joy of living your best life.

Break It Down

One way to ensure your leap gets off the ground is to become aware of the forces around you. The following action steps can help you develop that awareness both in football and in life.

FOOTBALL

1. Observe a football game and identify the offense with the ball making forward progress down the field. Notice how they move the ball a little bit at a time.

2. Watch for big-hearted moves where offensive players leap into action to create big plays.

3. Notice that plays don't always work out, yet the players get right back in and try again.

4. Observe the defense. Notice the strong will to stop the other side from making forward progress.

5. Where are the coaches? Are they on the field? Or are they on the sidelines observing?

6. When the players line up on the field, watch for the moment of calm before they snap the ball and leap into action.

LIFE

1. Acknowledge when you feel forward progress in your life. Write about it in your LIPSTICK FOOTBALL Journal. Any amount of forward progress is always a win—in football and in life.

2. Have you heard an inner hint or whisper about taking a leap toward something? If you write about it, it will become clearer and stronger.

3. Identify a personal project or goal you'd like to achieve as you work through the LIPSTICK Football principles. Remember, we will all benefit.

4. As you take offensive steps forward, observe whether something or someone is trying to pull you off course. That would be your defense.

5. Practice stepping back and putting on your coach's hat to observe, balance and coordinate your energetic forces.

6. Invite perspective. Is your three-legged stool in balance? If not, don't stare at the broken leg. Fix it and move on.

Chapter 3

IMMERSE

Suiting Up

Any fool can know. The point is to understand.

—Albert Einstein, Theoretical Physicist

I love hummingbirds. They're mini miracles. They're the only bird that can fly backwards—up, down, and sideways, for that matter. They might travel alone for 500 miles at a time. They don't have a sense of smell but can see color, which is why most hummingbird feeders are bright red. They can see farther than a human. The hummingbird brain, which is smaller than a pea, makes up approximately 4.2% of its body weight, the largest proportion in the bird kingdom. Their hearts beat 1,260 times a minute. And they weigh less than a nickel. A flock of hummingbirds is called, quite appropriately, a charm. A flock can also be referred to by other charming terms, such as a bouquet, a glittering, a hover, a shimmer or a tune.

These are just some interesting facts I've learned by reading and researching one of my favorite birds. I learned all this online in about five minutes. Yet that knowledge was enough to make me want to get a hummingbird feeder. Not knowing which one to get, I asked a friend for help. She said, "Come over and look at mine. And come at sunset." I felt a tad impatient and wanted to say, "Can't you just tell me what feeder to buy? Email me the link? I want to get started right away." Instead, I was polite and went to see her.

When I arrived just before sunset, my friend showed me her feeders, then started covering each one with a cloth. She pointed to two chairs close by and we sat down. I asked about the coverings and she explained that without access to a big feeder, the little hummers would look for other options to feed from in the same area.

Next, my friend asked me to put my thumb and forefinger together to form an "OK" signal. Then inside my horizontal "OK" she placed a handheld hummingbird feeder that fit there perfectly. "She's done this before," I thought. "In just a minute," she said, "hummingbirds will come and feed from the single feeder in your hand." I didn't believe it for a second.

I held the feeder very still and waited. It didn't take long before an iridescent green hummingbird settled gently on my finger in front of the solo feeder. In a whispered voice, my friend explained that this type of hummingbird was friendly, gentle. Watching this magnificent tiny beauty drink in front of me, from the perch of my finger, I observed every detail of what she was saying. Then a "Red Baron" hummer dive-bombed my hand to shoo away the shy green one. "This one's a bully," she said, as the red hummer forced its turn at the tiny trough.

Amazing! All my senses were happy and alert—seeing the hummers land, feeling their delicate feet on my own finger, hearing the rapid flapping of their wings, feeling the tiniest gusts of wind against my hand, and smelling the scent of sugar water in the air. Even the dive-bombing of the shy iridescent green beauty seemed like a dance—a *pas de deux* of Nature. I was deeply moved; no words could adequately describe that moment. In a single sitting,

I *knew* about hummingbirds. I understood them—not by reading about them; by experiencing them.

Introducing the I Principle — IMMERSE

Once you've taken a leap and decided to pursue your dream, you may at times feel like you're standing outside an invisible wall looking into what you want—whether that's to feed hummingbirds or change the world with your gifts and skills. When you immerse yourself in something, you get past that wall. You don't just learn *what*—you absorb *how* and *why*. You don't simply brush against knowledge mentally—you absorb it physically. That up close and personal perspective prepares you for your journey, shields your vulnerabilities, and aligns you more closely with your dream. It gives you a deeper and clearer sense of what you want and how you might get it.

How do you immerse? Be open. Be patient. Go where your heart leads you. Follow closely the path of your curiosities. And don't turn down offers from friends who have something exciting to share. By simply choosing to sit with my friend for a few minutes, I got to see what she saw and learn what she knew. I benefited from what she had already experienced. And it happened quickly. By immersing yourself in aspects of your journey, you could make a greater impact, and make it more effectively.

In this chapter, I'll talk about suiting up for a football game. I want you to understand how all players—both guys and gals—immerse and prepare *before* taking the field. You might think of suiting up as simply putting on a team's uniform. Although those designs and logos get more stylish and sophisticated all the time, that's simply the outer layer. Football, like life, is tough. Experienced players know they are vulnerable on the field. To protect themselves, they have to pay extra attention to what lies beneath that outer layer.

As you learn how football players suit up for a game, think about how you can prepare yourself for your next adventure. Don't just read about it. Don't just research it. Experience it. Be a student of life and feel the joy of learning. Take a field trip and absorb it. Find a mentor. Talk to an expert. Spend time with someone who has the experience you want, like my friend the hummingbird whisperer.

As I can attest from my time with the hummers, the richness and depth of your immersion will become a sustaining resource as you plot your course and journey down the field of life. (To see a video of me becoming a hummingbird whisperer, go to www.LipstickFootball.com/extras.)

The Football

Two sides and a ball. A football.

Before a game begins, football players take steps to immerse themselves—on the field and off. They suit up in uniform and protective gear, and they warm up on the field by tossing around the "pigskin," as the football is sometimes called. The term "pigskin" comes from football's older relative, rugby, which used a pig's bladder to create the inner part of the ball that holds air. The inner bladder is made from rubber today, but you'll still hear the old nickname now and then. The rough, pebbly exterior is made from cow's hide.

At 11 inches long and 22 inches around the middle, the official NFL football feels big in my hand. The Women's Professional Football League used college footballs, which follow NCAA standards (National Collegiate Athletic Association). NCAA balls are slightly smaller—about 1/2 to one inch shorter and an inch less around the circumference—yet weigh about the same, 14 to 15 ounces.

When you compare the NFL and NCAA footballs, you'll see the NCAA ball has a white stripe circling either end. The NFL football has no white stripes. The story goes that the white stripes helped players see the ball better when playing at night. At the time that decision was made, the NFL didn't have that many night games, so they chose not to add the white circular stripes. One thing they have in common is that Wilson is the official provider for both the NFL and NCAA footballs.

In this book, I'm using football as a template for how to view life, which makes the football itself pretty significant. To offensive football players, a football is precious. They want to hold on to it, to protect it. They want to get it downfield and into the end zone to score. Don't you want to protect your dream and make sure it gets into the end zone? Of course, you do. Why not use the football as a metaphor for your own dream or desire.

And since you're learning to immerse in this chapter, I highly recommend buying a "Goldilocks" football—one that feels good in *your* hands. After all, that's what immersion is all about—finding what fits you best and knowing why. So, get a football that feels good, then hold on tight! (You can find football suggestions in the "Break It Down" section at the end of this chapter.)

The Power of Suiting Up

Do you "dress for success?" Do you feel a mental uptick when you slip from a robe into meeting clothes? Does putting on a suit or jacket give you an air of authority you didn't have before?

Psychological studies suggest your choice of clothes impacts how you feel. Even wearing bright colors can pull you out of a funk. It's no wonder phrases like "dress for success," "dressed to the nines," and "dressed to kill" have been around so long. Even as far back as the Middle Ages, the educator Erasmus counseled teenagers with the phrase, "Clothes maketh the man."

It turns out, the right outfit doesn't just make you *feel* confident. A change of outfit can actually change your ability to perform. An experimental study on "Enclothed Cognition" at Northwestern University, by Adam Galinsky and Hajo Adam, found that when people put on a white lab coat, their cognitive abilities improved. Let me repeat that. People who put on a white medical coat actually tested smarter in that moment. I decided to perform a personal trial and ordered my own white lab coat. Guess what? When I wear it, I actually feel smarter, even if I'm just working at my computer.

The same is true in football. When I played women's tackle football, the moment I put on those protective shoulder pads, I was transformed. I felt tougher, stronger and more confident—even though I was still the same scrawny gal I was before suiting up. Do you think for an instant a professional football player would play a game without putting on their 20 pounds of uniform and protective gear? No way.

As I lead you through the various layers of protective gear, I encourage you to imagine yourself suiting up in a football uniform. Yes, you—in a football uniform. If you tried one on, at least in your mind, I think you would feel differently about the game. You'd understand how pads soften the blows of physical contact. How cleats let you dig into the field to hold your position or create better traction to run faster. How wearing a helmet might limit the way you see the game.

Of course, suiting up is a metaphor for immersion. When you take the time to immerse yourself in a subject or skill, it prepares you for action—mentally and physically. It boosts your confidence and raises your performance level, just like wearing a white doctor's coat. Now, that's powerful stuff. Maybe it's time for you to prepare for your own game and "dress" for your own success. Even if you decide against the white doctor's coat.

Let's suit up!

Under the Hood

The foundation of protective gear includes padded pants and shoulder pads. But what's under that? Undies. Players typically wear as their base layer a type of undershirt called half tees, which are short-sleeve T-shirts that come just below the ribs. Following the same concept as a woman's camisole, these shirts provide a protective layer next to the player's skin, so the heavy shoulder pads won't chafe or scratch, and they're short enough not to restrict movement around the waist. In cold weather, players often wear long-sleeve half-tees.

For protection of their privates, guys wear a modified jockstrap with a thick foam pad to create a soft cup. A hard cup like baseball players wear wouldn't provide the mobility you need in football to push and shove and run and jump. Gals who play the game have their own special protection, which I'll cover later in this chapter.

Moving down, the next stop of undergarments is socks, or their more official name, stockings. Football stockings are sort of like gals' knee-high hosiery, only thicker. They go over the calf right up to the base of the knee. Newer socks are massively engineered—light-weight nylon and acrylic, cushioned on the bottom of the foot to help reduce shock. They can also have a reinforced toe area, arch support, and side air vents.

With so many features in these undergarments, you might think Q was developing them for James Bond.

Protective Pants

Remember bumper cars? You drive around in a small plastic car just large enough to sit in, and ram into other cars swerving in all directions. Putting on the next layer of protective gear—padded pants and shoulder pads—is like wearing a bumper car. They give players the freedom to perform while protecting the vulnerable areas of their body.

Padded pants may remind you of an old-fashioned woman's girdle. In fact, these padded underpants are actually referred to as girdles. Standard girdles have slots or pockets like envelopes, similar to the shoulder pad pockets in some women's blouses. There are typically seven pockets—two knees, two thighs, two hip bones, and one tail bone. It's easier if the pads go in the slots before the pants go on the player. At least it was for me. You'll also find integrated pants where the pads are permanently attached.

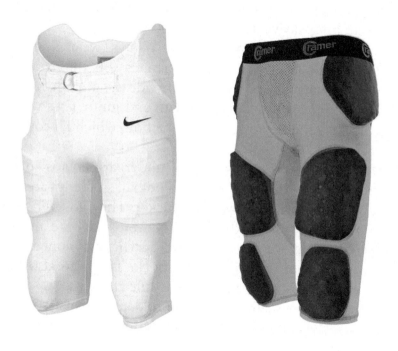

Slotted padded pants and integrated padded pants

As football players immerse themselves in their positions, they develop a keen awareness of the padding thickness that will serve them best. For example, players who block or tackle from a more stationary position might choose thicker pads for extra thigh and hip bone protection. Players who need to run fast to catch a ball might choose thinner pads for more flexibility. However they're configured, the purpose of padded underpants is to protect the vulnerable parts of a football player's body.

When you immerse yourself into an area of interest, you, too, will develop a keen awareness of the details surrounding you. That thorough familiarity will guide you to make choices that will benefit and protect you as you move forward on your journey.

The Blessed Shoulder Pads

Nothing says "football player" quite like shoulder pads. You can take a 4-foot nothing, 90 pound 12-year-old who looks like a spaghetti strand, put shoulder pads on her, and miraculously—a football player is born. Speaking from experience, after lacing up my shoulder pads and hitting the field, I felt tougher, stronger, and mightier than before.

Me—decked out in my practice uniform with shoulder pads

But it's not just how a player looks on the outside or feels on the inside. Those shoulder pads have a purpose—to soften the hits on the field. The shoulder pads sit atop your shoulders and extend down to protect your chest. The pads open up in the middle, allowing the left and right sides to expand, making it easy to pull over your head. Once on your shoulders, the two sides are connected in place by two garter-like elastic bands that come from the back and hook onto the front—securing the shoulder pads and keeping them from slipping or twirling around your neck.

Most shoulder pads are pretty equal in purpose and use. However, some are lighter and cut thinner around the rib cage to allow for more flexibility and movement.

Narrow-cut shoulder pads for players who need to run or throw

For example, players who run or throw the football can't afford to be weighed down and constricted by a heavy bulky corset. But those who don't have to run, who just need to stand and block runners from getting past them, often need more protection in their chest and rib area.

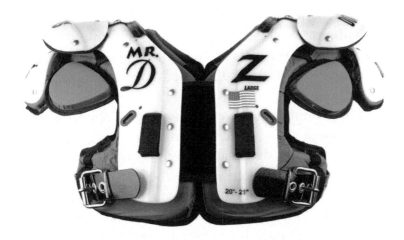

Wide-cut shoulder pads for non-running players

Speaking of protection, there are shoulder pads designed specifically for female players. To protect a woman's breast area, molded plastic cups are attached to the shoulder harness of the pads. Like the men's version, these pads have to be put on over your head and then laced together like an old corset.

Shoulder pads are made of foam rubber, elastics, and the kind of durable, shock-resistant plastics perfected for auto assembly lines. It's almost like players are wearing cars over their bodies. Sort of like, well, bumper cars.

Neck protection is very important to players, especially those who are vulnerable to getting hit midair by leaping up to catch the ball. Those players attach an additional support onto their shoulder pads that protects their necks from whiplash types of moves and jolts.

Learning about protective gear is a good opportunity to put your inner coach to work identifying your own vulnerabilities. Where are you exposed? What are your weak links? Do you need to bolster hard skills for your job, maybe learn another computer program? Are there opportunities you have always wanted to explore but haven't yet? When you immerse, you'll learn new things, and at a deeper level, which might give you as much advantage on your field as shock-resistant protective gear gives football players.

Jerseys and Pants

You've tackled the protective layers. Let's finish dressing by putting on the pants and jersey you actually see players wear. How the name *jersey* came to be used for this part of the uniform is a long but fun story. I'll keep it short. A United Kingdom (UK) island called Jersey was famous for making wool sweaters. The sweaters were tightly knit and worn by seamen to keep them warm. In the 1890s, they found their way to the U.S. and to American football. Before players started using the heavy-duty shoulder pads, teams used the jersey sweaters to add a layer of protection. Voilà—jerseys.

The design of a football jersey is quite slimming actually. It has to be broad at the top to cover the shoulder pads and slim at the waste to tuck into the pants. Some players like their jersey to be skintight around the chest and waist area so, during a game, it's harder for another player to grab them.

The football jersey says a lot about a player. It identifies the player's last name, team and position. The NFL has rules about the size of the numbers and letters and their location on a jersey. A player's name on the back of the jersey has to be 2.5 inches tall and a player's number has to be 8 inches tall by 4 inches wide. Did you know that your football jersey number also indicates the position you're playing? More about that in chapter 5.

With 22 players on the field at any given time, it's helpful to have contrasting light and dark color schemes to distinguish between the two teams. NFL allows the home team to choose their jersey color and the visiting team wears the opposite. According to Cory Befort, Sr. Creative Director for the Los Angeles Rams, "Designated *home* jerseys typically favor in sales to fans more than *away* jerseys."

Two sets of Los Angeles Rams uniforms (light and dark)

Cory is currently working on expanding the Rams uniform set beyond the standard *home* and *away* designations. "My goal is to provide more options to players *and* fans by offering a variety of appealing jerseys that may be worn at home games." Currently, the Rams don't designate a dark or light primary uniform as their home or away selection and instead, prior to the start of the season, allow players to choose what they want to wear each week.

Covering the protective padded pants is yet another pair of pants. At the waist is a tie band. The bottom of the pants, which usually stop just below the knees, also has ties to snug them into place. Tall matching socks or stockings complete the outfit.

Every aspect of the NFL uniform—pants and jersey color, pad thickness, sock color, shoe and shoelace color, logo placement, number size, towel placement, wristbands, headbands—is scrutinized by the NFL Uniform Inspector. Starting a few hours before each game, the Uniform Inspector watches pre-game warmups and visits locker rooms to examine uniforms and accessories. According to the NFL, the purpose of this scrutiny, which continues throughout the game, is "to protect players from injury, maintain competitive balance, create a professional appearance and protect the league's business partnerships."

The Helmet

When you watch football on TV, you see a combination of camera shots—close-ups of players, bird's-eye views of the field and an overhead fly-by Skycam feed of break-out runs and catches. When you attend a football game in person, you can take in the entire field with your peripheral vision.

Football players, however, are not so lucky. They see the game through their helmet's face mask—also called a *grill* or *cage*. It takes getting used to, and certainly doesn't compare to what viewers see watching action on a 4K television monitor, but "a view through a grill" is the way every player on the field sees and experiences the game.

A player's view of the game hasn't always been so limited. In the early days of football, helmets weren't even required. Although the views may have been good, there were numerous head injuries. Finally, in 1943, the NFL required players to wear leather helmets, updating them a decade later to the plastic polymer helmets and face masks we see today.

Face masks come in two basic categories. Let's simplify the positions into blockers and runners, as we did with shoulder pads. Blockers don't move far from their original starting positions, so they don't need a lot of visibility down the field. Instead, they need a helmet cage with several bars to protect them from hands and fingers flying and flailing around their face and eyes.

Runners and throwers will have a helmet grill with fewer bars providing a wider field of vision so they can see where they're running or throwing.

Blocker grill vs quarterback or receiver grill

Kickers have an especially difficult time. When they look down to kick the ball, it's like looking through bifocals. They have to tilt their helmet just right to see the ball on the field. Some players wear visors or eye shields attached to their grills. Like giant sunglasses, these filter glare and provide additional protection for their eyes or nose. To secure the helmet, a plastic chinstrap snaps onto either side.

I'll never forget when we fitted helmets for my women's football team. Trainers used screwdrivers, pliers, and air pumps to fit them just right. They would push pieces of Styrofoam padding inside for a snug fit, attach the appropriate grill for the position each woman was playing, and then adjust the strap. Just when you thought the helmet couldn't get tighter, the equipment manager fit the thin needle of the air pump into the top of the helmet and started pumping until the helmet felt almost painfully tight. That's when you knew it was actually going to protect you.

Helmets keep evolving; leading manufacturers utilize every advance in materials design to make them better at absorbing shock and protecting against concussions. They're high tech, too.

A few key players on the field wear helmets outfitted with a tiny speaker. When you see a player place a hand over his helmet ear as though listening to the ocean in a shell, he's really listening to a coach send in the next play. If you can catch a glimpse of the back of that player's helmet, you will see a small NFL green dot indicating it's a radio helmet.

And last but not least, helmet style. Leave it to Los Angeles to bring a little Hollywood marketing to football. In 1948, the Los Angeles Rams got the idea to put its logo on their helmets. Today, every NFL team–with the exception of the Cleveland Browns–has their team logo on their helmets. And the Browns logo *is* their helmet.

Los Angeles Rams Helmet and Logo – 1989 and 2021

Accessories

Have you immersed yourself enough in the football uniform to "hit the field," as they say—at least in your mind? Not so fast. Don't forget the accessories. While some accessories maximize a player's safety, some simply reflect a personal preference.

The Mouthguard

A mouthguard is like a plastic tooth whitening tray that fits under your upper teeth. Although the NFL does not require players to wear one, many players do to protect against grinding or chipping their teeth during play. A mouthguard also cushions blows that might cause concussions, cerebral hemorrhages, or even neck injuries. To make sure they don't go missing, mouthguards often come with a plastic string-like connector that attaches to a helmet grill around the mouth area. You'll also see players push their mouthguard into a crevice on their helmet as a temporary resting spot.

Shoes with Spikes

In case you're new to all field sports, cleats are athletic shoes with spikes attached to the soles. Cleats give a player traction as they move or run on the field. The spikes can be rubberized and molded onto the shoe, or they can be short metal spikes that screw into the shoe's sole.

The screw-in variety allows players the flexibility to swap them out for a different type or length depending on field and weather conditions. For example, when it's raining cats and dogs on a grassy field, you want claws that grip like the animals themselves.

Eye Black

Somewhat unique to American football is the wearing of a type of functional makeup called "eye black." Eye black is simply grease made of beeswax, paraffin, and carbon. Players apply the black grease beneath their eyes to reduce glare from direct sunlight or stadium lights. Some players apply anti-glare stickers beneath their eyes that do the same thing as the grease. The stickers often display team colors or a logo.

Gloves

Some players like to wear gloves, and some don't. Depending on the weather, football gloves can really help a player hang on to the ball or throw it more accurately. When players use their hands to block other players, gloves add additional protection for their fingers. Unlike other more generic accessories, football gloves are made for specific positions or activities.

Huddle Up

As players suit up and immerse themselves in their role on the team, they make personal choices about comfort and protection. Some players like to wear eye black or a helmet visor. But they have no say in some things such as uniform standards and design. Those decisions are made for them.

When you step into your own project or goals, you need to clarify and balance what you can control and what you can't. Immersion gives you that insight. Like the effect of a helmet grill on a player's view, immersing yourself will allow you to start to see your target space differently and make the best choices for yourself moving forward.

Break It Down

To immerse is to give yourself an opportunity to experience something with your senses, going beyond just learning facts. Work through this list to immerse yourself in football and in life.

FOOTBALL

1. Owning your own football is a great way to immerse yourself in the game. I recommend purchasing a "Goldilocks" football—one that fits comfortably in your hand. My hand is not that big and tossing around a Junior-sized football is comfortable for me. (www.LipstickFootball.com/extras)

2. Pick a player or two and look at their jersey information. What's the player's name? Number?

3. Try to look through the jersey and imagine the shoulder pads and padded pants beneath the uniform.

4. What accessories do you see the players wearing? Mouthguard? Eye black? Gloves?

5. Which player's helmet has a green dot pasted on its back? What does that mean?

LIFE

1. Think about what it means to suit up in your own life. To prepare yourself for what's to come and get ready to hit the field. Don't forget to write your thoughts in your journal.

2. As you think about what you want to do, achieve or become, identify specific ways you can immerse yourself in your goal. Is there a skill you can develop? Is there someone who could mentor you?

3. Use your football as a metaphor for your goal. Throughout the day, pick it up and toss it around or just hold it. You are in control of your journey. And holding on to the football will remind you of that.

4. Want to conduct an experiment on boosting your brain power? Consider wearing your very own white lab coat.

Chapter Four

PLAY

Hitting the Field

John Kinsella: Is this heaven?

Ray Kinsella: It's—it's Iowa.

John: I could have sworn it was heaven.

Ray: Is there a heaven?

John: Oh yeah. It's the place where dreams come true.

Ray: Maybe this is heaven.

In the 1989 movie *Field of Dreams*, Kevin Costner plays an Iowan corn farmer, Ray Kinsella, who hears a voice: "If you build it, he will come." Ray, a huge baseball fan, cuts down his cornfield and builds a baseball diamond in hopes of bringing back an old player, Shoeless Joe, who died years before. And it works. Joe comes back and plays on Ray's magical field of dreams. But that wasn't the "he" meant by the voice Ray heard. Building the baseball field also brings back Ray's father, John. Getting to play pitch and catch again with his now-deceased father is something Ray had not imagined.

This chapter is all about taking the field—getting to know the place football players go to tackle their opponents and make their athletic dreams come true. It's also about playing in your own field of dreams. There's a beauty to an empty field. Before the first practice. Before the first kick. Without the roar of a crowd. Like a blank canvas, an empty field welcomes a player to imagine what it would be like to put her skills and training into action. To make her dreams come true.

So often, when you set your sights on a dream, you expect yourself to shift immediately to your goals and get down to business. You go to work, draw up a plan, or start a task list, and before you know it, you're exhausted from the weight of those expectations. You say to yourself, "Maybe now is not the time to pursue my dreams. I'll set this one aside and try again later." Then BAM—the door slams on that tiny opening where you felt motivated to take a leap, to pursue your dream, and that dream disappears before you even take the field.

I used to make this shift from dream to goal really fast. I even thought the two words were synonymous—interchangeable, though dressed differently. Dreams were fairy dust and make-believe. Goals were businesslike, with an action plan and "To Do" list. But dreams and goals are not the same. Dreams can be fragile and ephemeral. They need time and space to develop. To grow without fear of an opponent coming down hard on them, especially if that opponent is you. They need time to solidify—and become real.

How do you protect your dream? How do you defend it against challengers on the field of life? Let's remember what you do on a field and what the field is called. A football field is called, as it is in many sports, a *playing* field. And you go to the field to do what? *Play* ball.

Introducing the P principle — PLAY

Everyone knows how important playing is for children. Through play, children develop language skills and learn problem solving, social interaction, creative self-expression and teamwork. They nurture their imagination through games of make-believe. I remember building a "kid cave" in the roof trusses and rafters of my family's garage that allowed me to magically transform into a trapeze artist. "Child's play" literally shapes and forms young brains by developing neural pathways that help tackle more complex issues in the future.

Fast forward—and you're all grown up. Is play any less important for you now than it was for you as a child? Studies show that adults reduce stress when they play, boost lung function, strengthen their heart and trigger endorphins. And there's more. Psychiatrist Stuart Brown, founder of the National Institute for Play in Carmel Valley, CA, says in a Washington Post article by Jennifer Wallace, "What all play has in common is that it offers a sense of engagement and pleasure, takes the player out of a sense of time and place, and the experience of doing it is more important than the outcome."

What Dr. Brown said about adult play sounds a little like make-believe to me. After all, make-believe takes the player away from "time and place," i.e., reality. Where "the experience of doing it is more important than the outcome." That's exactly why you separate dreams from goals. Remember, a goal is something you plot out and track. It's *how* you bring a dream into reality. We'll get to tracking goals soon enough. But first, you have a critical job to do—loosen your grip on reality and embrace the joy of playing and dreaming.

As you get to know the football field in this chapter, I want you to create your own dreamscape—that place in your heart, mind or mind's eye where your dreams can come true. Play and frolic on your field. Go there often. If you like a particular dreamscape scenario, replay it over and over again. Dress it up, make it outrageous, flamboyant. Be silly. And be brave. Know your dream and own it. The more outside of normal you imagine your dream, with you in it, the easier time your brain will have accessing the neural pathway to review it again and again. Until one day, that dream will become your reality.

When you set your goals and make a plan, then blow the whistle to start your game clock, will you get knocked down? Yes, of course. But will you leave the field? If you're a stranger on that field, if you don't feel you own it, you might leave. But if you've dreamed your fondest dream on that field and fueled it with a ton of passion as Ray did, and as football players do, if you've walked every nook and cranny and know where all the gems of your dream are hidden, you could get knocked down all day long and you'd simply pick yourself back up—and keep playing.

The Playing Field

The American football playing field is big—about 57,600 square feet or 1.32 acres of land. Plenty of room for walking and dreaming, listening to your heart and entertaining your options. Mark the field with hundreds of white lines and you have what looks more like a road map with mile markers to a specific destination.

Football players may warm up by walking the field and dreaming of a Super Bowl win. But when it's game time, then like you, they want to conquer that field—yard by yard. Before you can conquer something, you have to know it. In the last chapter, I asked you to buy a football and start tossing it around. Now I want you to put on your sneakers, grab your ball, jump the fence if you have to, and go explore a football field. Ready? Let's hit it.

Working your way from the outside in, at most local high school and college football fields you'll see a running track circling the field. Circle the field four times and you've run a mile. After you've run your mile, or at least walked once around for your quarter-mile warm-up (500 steps), walk to a corner and look down the field toward the other end. Can you even see it clearly? It's quite a distance. That's why it takes several tries for a team to get the ball from one end to the other to score.

If you take time to walk over and around a football field, you will see the field the way a player sees it. Its expanse is freeing—the perfect place to stimulate a dream, whether athletic or artistic. Yet the field is highly organized with lots of white lines, marks and numbers. While getting into the end zone to score is the ultimate goal, in football and in life, you don't have to rush to get there, especially when you're nurturing a dream.

Personally, I experience a deep calm when I work within a structured environment. As you walk the playing field, let it provide a gentle structure in your own thinking about what you want, what you're dreaming about. Let it represent your path laid out as a direct linear course and know that what you want can be measured and tracked. Know this is where you will shine and initiate plays. Catch the ball and run. And kick ass all up and down your field of dreams. You'll cover these important principles soon. But first, your heart's desire has to be dreamed and imagined. And perhaps tickled.

While the focus of this book is on American football, its rules and regulations, the game is played in other countries, including Canada, Mexico, New Zealand, Australia, European countries and even Africa and Egypt. Game rules and field dimensions may vary in other countries.

Grass or Turf

Friday night lights and the smell of fresh-cut grass. Ahhh. At most high schools throughout America, that's exactly what you'd experience on a Fall Friday night. My high school was no different. Although I didn't play on the football team as some gals do today (see chapter 9), I marched in my high school band (Go Marshall Rams!) on that newly cut grassy field. Even in women's professional tackle football, I played on a grass field. Is that why the smell of fresh-cut grass is so powerful to me and other players? It makes sense. If you're doing something you love, and you smell fresh-cut grass as you're doing it, that association will create a positive connection in your brain.

Grass is one choice for a football field surface. The other one, of course, is artificial turf. The first use of artificial turf was in 1966 at the Astrodome in Houston, TX. The Astrodome was an indoor stadium where growing grass wasn't feasible. Artificial grass was chosen as the alternative. After the product became popular, the company that produced it, Monsanto, rebranded it after the name of the stadium, and the new name stuck—AstroTurf.

AstroTurf required very little maintenance, so why it became popular is easy to understand. Although unrealistically stiff and shiny in the beginning, the turf was soon produced to look and feel pretty close to the real thing. Today there are newer and more advanced versions of artificial or synthetic turf. Of all the NFL teams, a little more than half use a synthetic turf.

Studies have tried to determine which surface produces fewer football injuries. As you might imagine, with the variances of weather, players' abilities, and other factors, the results were never crystal clear. In a 2010 NFL Players Association survey, about 82 percent of the players felt artificial turf triggered more injuries than natural grass. Still, many outdoor stadiums are equipped with it because it's easier to maintain under a variety of conditions. But sadly, they can't reproduce the "fresh-cut grass" smell.

Yard Lines

A football field is measured. It's so beautifully organized it mirrors itself both lengthwise and across. That means if you learn just one quarter of it, you'll understand the entire field. The primary playing area of a football field is 100 yards long and 53 1/3 yards wide (300 feet by 160 feet). Capping off each end are even more yards where play occurs at certain times throughout the game. We'll get to those in a minute.

If you position yourself at a far-end corner, then walk onto the field, you'll cross over a six-inch white painted line that marks the outer edge of the entire playing area. Segmenting the long field are horizontal lines across its width that mark five-yard increments. Each white line is four inches wide, not quite as wide as the outline around the entire field. Every other line represents ten yards and is labeled with a number—10, 20, 30, 40 and so on. It's easy to see the yard-line numbers because they measure six feet from bottom to top. I'm 5'4" so a number would extend past my head if I lay down beside it.

Notice the 10-yard numbers start 10 yards in from the goal line at one end of the field, advance to the center 50-yard line, then descend toward the goal line at the opposite end of the field. The reason the yard-line numbers don't go from 0 to 100 is that each team "owns" and protects one half of the field. The goal of football is to cross into your opponents' side or territory and move the ball across their goal line to score.

There are two sets of 10-yard numbers, one on each side of the field. If you drew a vertical line down the middle of the field and put up a mirror, you would see that the 10-yard markings are the same. They face opposite directions so stadium fans on both sides can read the ball location easily from a distance. Look closely at those 10-yard numbers and you will see a large triangular arrow pointing to the closest end of the field.

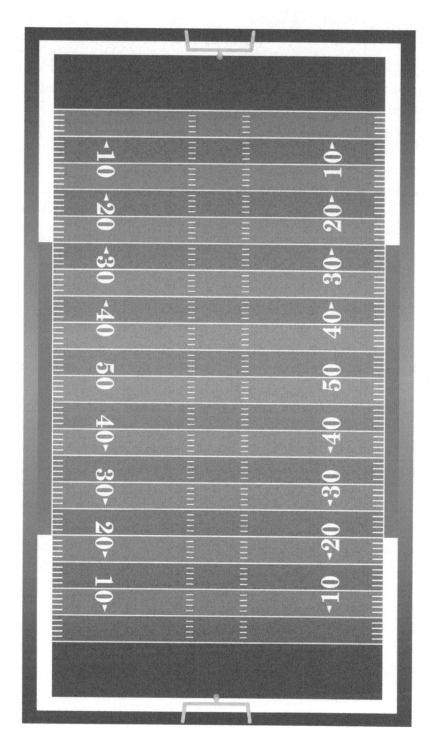

Originally, the white lines and numbers were made with white chalk. Can you imagine the mess created by players running over the chalk lines? Or what a hard rain might do to them? Today, the white markings are painted onto the field.

Hash Marks

It's time for you to take strides and pace the field. Start on the white edge of the field outline at the 10-yard line and look down. To your left and right running all along the edge of the field are a hundred short white lines, called hash marks, marking one-yard increments.

Interestingly, the etymology of the word hash comes from the French word haché or hacher and means to "hack or chop into small pieces." That might bring to mind a hatchet that chops or chopped-up hashed browned potatoes. Service stripes that represent rank on a military uniform are also called hash marks.

Now, test your stride against those hash marks on the football field. You'll probably be able to reach a five-yard line with about five giant steps. Pick up the pace and jog five yards. As you put motion behind it, is it easier to hit those five yards? Next, give yourself ten or 20 yards to build up some steam and try a flat-out run. When football players run downfield with the ball, they can cover five yards in a few big strides.

Next, move to the 50-yard line and walk toward the center of the field. Before you get to the center, you'll see another row of yard marks going from one end of the field to the other. Actually, there are two rows—about 18.5 feet apart. And if you walk to the other side of the field, you'll see the one-yard line markings again. Remember, a football field cut down the middle mirrors itself. Did you catch the team's logo in the middle of the field on the 50-yard line? Not all fields have one, but most do.

Think that's a lot of field markings? It's nothing compared to what football fields used to look like. Introducing...the *gridiron*. That term has been used in American football circles over the years and still is today. Then, the football playing field looked a lot like a checkerboard or gridiron.

Football stadium at Syracuse University (1910) showing original grid pattern

In 1920, when American football became its own sport, the old gridiron pattern was changed to the more open plan of today. I don't know about you, but I'll take bold white six-foot numbers and directional arrows any day of the week.

The End Zone

Capping each end of the football playing field is a 10-yard-deep section of the field called the end zone. In college football fields and some professional ones, end zones are painted with a team's colors and logos. Besides running across the goal line with the ball, a team can score a touchdown by catching the ball inside the end zone. A deep end-zone catch can be one of the most dramatic and athletic plays of a football game. The move you finesse to get your dream into the end zone might be a match for it.

Outlining each end zone are four rectangular markers called pylons. Two pylons sit on either end of the goal line and two sit in the back corners of the end zone. The four pylons create a boundary or parameter for players to see peripherally as they move into the end zone to score.

A pylon is made of bright orange plastic and is flexible enough so that a player can fall on it and not get hurt. At least by the pylon (a pile-on by other players is a different matter). During a televised game, you may see a replay from a small pylon camera that captures "close-call" plays along the goal line.

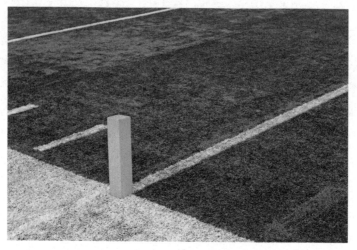

One of four pylons that outline the end zone

At the back edge of the end zone, centered between the sidelines, is the goalpost, which looks something like a square metal slingshot. It has a single arched vertical post that supports a horizontal crossbar and two vertical posts rising up to the sky.

Kicking a football over the crossbar and between the two upright posts is how a team scores extra points. You may hear of a kicker who "split the uprights." That means she kicked a ball in between the two vertical bars of that U-shaped goalpost. High school and some college football fields may still use the older style goal post that stands straight up like a giant "H"—with two straight vertical bars and a horizontal crossbar connecting them in the middle.

The 20 yards leading up to each end zone is referred to as the "red zone." It's not really red, it's green like the rest of the field. However, once a team gets the ball this close to the goal line, things start to heat up. A team may bring the ball down the field quickly and easily but then choke and stall under pressure when they get to these last 20 yards.

Once you start to bring your own dream downfield, stay alert to the point when you reach the red zone. You may need extra support, or you may need to recall those initial supercharged visions of your dream to help propel you over the goal line.

The Scoreboard

Throughout a football game, spectators' and players' eyes search for a scoreboard—a quick reference to see who's leading and how much game time is left. You might take scoreboards for granted because they've always been there. Haven't they?

No, because in the early years of professional football, teams often shared a field with baseball teams. But baseball teams don't play to a running clock. They play nine innings no matter how long it takes. For a football game, officials were given the task of keeping track of time. Over the years, as football became a bigger sport and teams could afford a dedicated field, they added clocks to their scoreboards to track time of play.

The scoreboard displays a lot of information, starting at the top with scores for home team vs. guest team. Other information includes current quarter of play, which team has possession of the ball, current down and remaining yards, and ball location—all of which is constantly updated throughout the game.

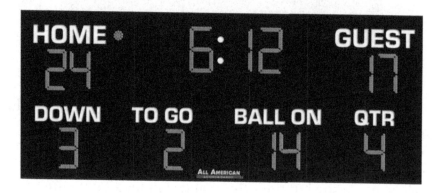

Bigger stadiums have several large video monitors that show replays or live action of the game. Since players can't see themselves in action, you will often see them look up at the video screen with as much interest as the fans to see the results of their efforts.

At the end of the field against a back wall is another time device similar to a very large timer. It's called a play clock. When it's active, you'll see it count down from 40 seconds, which is the amount of time a team has between plays to organize and initiate its next play.

The play clock is huge and is pretty close to eye level. Players on the 50-yard line can look up and read it easily. They can even see it out of the corner of their eye, which is important. If a team doesn't initiate a play within the allotted 40 seconds of prep time, they'll be penalized.

The Bench Area

Not everyone on the team can be on the field at the same time. Where are non-active, injured or special skilled players when they're not playing? On the bench. On a football field there's a bench area for each team. Like the mirrored markings on the playing field, the two bench areas mirror each other in placement, size and markings. Positioned outside the sidelines of the playing field, each bench area covers a 30-yard length of field that straddles the 50-yard line.

If you want to get to know the bench area, find the 50-yard line and walk off the field past the sideline. But watch out! This is a restricted area reserved for players who run out-of-bounds to end a play and for officials who need to mark the new position of the ball. It's so important to protect this outer sideline space that, in 2010, the NFL asked each team to appoint a "get-back" coach whose job it is to simply make sure no one on the team or staff is hovering in that area. If a coach interferes with the official by wandering into that space, a team can be penalized.

Walk past the restricted area and you'll step into a six-foot deep area outlined with a broken white line. This is the coaching box, where coaches pace back and forth, confer and track game activity. It's also where substitute players stand so they can be ready to jump in and take another player's place at a moment's notice. Continue past the coaching box toward the benches. Careful you don't trip over the water bottles and other equipment in your way. This is where players sit and watch the game.

Remember the three-legged stool in chapter 2? Aren't you the coach of your own team? Sometimes it's necessary to step into the coach's box and allow your dream to simmer—as you season it with even greater detail and understanding.

Game Time

The official playing time for a football game is 60 minutes— just one hour. I know what you're thinking. If that's the case, then why does it take three or four hours on a Sunday afternoon to finish a game? Good question.

A 60-minute football game is divided into four quarters, each being 15 minutes of playing time. After the second quarter, the teams leave the field and head to their locker room for a 12-minute "halftime" break. College games take a 20-minute halftime, and the once-a-year big Super Bowl halftime, with its entertainment extravaganza, can last for 30 minutes.

For the most part, what you see during halftime on a television broadcast is typically a recap by network sports commentators of the first-half play—which players performed well and which fell short of expectations. What goes on in the locker rooms during halftime is an entirely different story.

Of course, players refuel by gulping fluids and wolfing down snacks. Trainers give banged-up players medical attention. Some players adjust pads and equipment or replace parts altogether. If the weather has changed and the field is slippery, they might replace their cleats. And in the few minutes they have together, coaches tweak their game plan and dial in a more effective strategy based on what they've seen from the opponent so far.

Keeping track of game time is official football business. You're not quite there yet. You're still using the football field as a metaphor to play and dream your boldest dream. When you're ready to transition your dream into a goal, know you can start that game clock and use those field markings to find your way into the end zone.

Professional Stadiums

AT&T. FedEx. Heinz. Bank of America. Mercedes Benz. Levis. Nissan.

What do these companies have in common? If you said football, you'd be right. These are just some of the companies who have purchased "naming rights" to an NFL stadium. In fact, most stadiums where NFL football is played have sold naming rights to corporations. As of 2020, only five of the leagues 30 stadiums have not—Lambeau Field (Green Bay Packers), Paul Brown Stadium (Cincinnati Bengals), Soldier Field (Chicago Bears), Arrowhead Stadium (Kansas City Chiefs) and the Bills Stadium (Buffalo Bills).

All stadiums are pretty big. They do, after all, have to house a 120-yard rectangular football field. But some have a greater seating capacity than others. The Chicago Bears play in the smallest stadium, Soldier Field, which has a seating capacity of 61,500. By comparison, the Dallas Cowboys, who play in the AT&T Stadium in Arlington, TX, get to hear the screams of over 100,000 fans.

Most stadiums are roofless and don't stay open year-round. A handful of stadiums have retractable roofs and a few have fixed roofs. Outdoor home teams in colder states use their open roof to their advantage. They build endurance to playing football outside in the snow. When opponents from sunnier climates come to play, the sun lovers don't do nearly as well.

A football field, and the stadium or seating area that surrounds it, creates a unique set of circumstances not just for team players but also for the fans that support them. When I think of playing football, I think of being outside on a grassy field, throwing the ball. When I think of watching the game, if it's in person, I like being low and close, not on the top row surrounded by 99,999 other people.

Huddle Up

I hope you've enjoyed your walking tour of a football field. Before you leave the field, before I start putting players in their positions and getting you into the action of a football game, think once again about your dream. Think about what you want, about your heart's desire.

Whether you get the opportunity to walk an actual football field or just take a walk around the block in your neighborhood, spend time mentally adding detail to your dream. Get to know it the same way you got to know the football field—one yard at a time. When the defense starts coming at you, you can stand strong—or know which way to run—in order to score.

Break It Down

A football field is an expansive area to dream. When you're ready, overlay the structure of the field onto your own journey or project. A goal line targets your focus; hash marks track progress; a game clock marks time; and a play clock sparks your actions.

FOOTBALL

1. Find a local football field you can walk on. Is the surface real grass or synthetic? Walk around a bit or take a little jog. How does the surface feel to you when you zig and zag?

2. As you walk along a sideline, see how your stride matches the one-yard markings. When you jog or run, how many strides does it take to reach from one five-yard line to the next?

3. Walk the perimeter of one of the end zones. Where is the goal post located? Are there pylons? Notice the thick white goal line. What yard number does the goal line represent?

4. If you can, take your football to a field and have some fun. Try kicking the ball. Run with it. How far can you throw it? Use the hash marks to mark the distance of your throw.

5. Scoreboards display team points. On television, the score appears in a lower third—with the visiting team listed on the left and the home team on the right. Who is the home team of the game you're watching?

LIFE

1. Where do you dream your dreams? A place in your heart or mind? Have you also found a spacious empty field or park that invites you to have fun playing with your dream?

2. As you spend time with your dream, can you make it bolder or add more detail to it? You want your dream to be clear and unforgettable, easy to recall and defend.

3. One day, you will want to get your dream across the goal line. Do you know your playing field well enough to make forward progress? To defend your dream moving downfield?

4. Want to put yourself into action? Set a timer for 40 seconds, the amount of time a football offense has to put their next play

into motion. Press Start. You have 40 seconds to decide on an action—and initiate it.

5. A football game is four quarters of 15 minutes each. You can accomplish a lot in that time. Set a timer for 15 minutes to enjoy and cultivate your dream.

Chapter 5

SHINE

Player Positions

A musician must make music, an artist must paint,
a poet must write, if [she] is to be ultimately at
peace with [herself].

—Abraham Maslow, American Psychologist

Hook 'Em, Horns! If you recognize that saying, you're either a University of Texas Longhorns alumni, a UT fan or a savvy sportster. When I say it, it fills me with pride and takes me back to my days marching in the University of Texas Longhorn Band. We played "The Eyes of Texas" as we marched up and down the field, making gigantic human wheels and stepping "six to five"—six steps to every five yards. We wore white cowboy hats, and we were cool.

The leader of the Longhorn Band at that time was a living legend known to band members simply as "Mr. D"—short for the now-deceased Mr. Vincent R. DiNino. Mr. D. was small but mighty! During his 30 years as the band director, he integrated the all-white, all-male band by opening it to all students, allowing me to become the first woman baritone horn player.

Mr. D wanted one thing from us. He wanted our best—whether we were on the field practicing, providing halftime entertainment during a national championship, or marching in the Cotton Bowl parade in Dallas, Texas. He gave each player a ton of respect. And he expected the same in return. As a result of every individual's hard work and his focused determination, he created a cohesive whole—and we shined. We shined individually, and we shined as a performing group.

Introducing the S Principle — SHINE

Have you ever shined? I hope you have. Abraham Maslow earned recognition as the father of humanistic psychology because he observed and taught that all human beings possess the same needs, though we are all differently and uniquely gifted, and that our basic needs (e.g., for safety and love) must be met before we can even recognize what will enable us to shine. In other words, there is a hierarchy of needs. A person's highest-level needs are to express her full potential.

Maslow found that on the way up the hierarchy, some people experienced truly extraordinary moments, little life highs, which he referred to as "peak experiences." For me, marching in the UT Longhorn Band was a peak experience. It was significant. It lifted me up and fulfilled me. I got to experience, at least for a short time, my best self.

According to Maslow, a peak experience includes three characteristics:

1) Significance – the experience has to mean something to you, give you an increased awareness. Maybe it's a turning point in your life.

2) Fulfillment – Peak experiences generate positive emotions and are intrinsically rewarding. They make you feel good all over.

3) Spiritual – During a peak experience you feel one

with the world, in flow, and sometimes lose track of time.

After learning about peak experiences, I started looking for other times in my life when I'd felt high on life. I discovered that, as when actively seeking grounds for many good things—such as gratitude and positive thinking—the more I searched my memory for peak experiences, the more I recalled. And needless to say, I experienced a few peak moments playing women's professional football.

Unfortunately, as much as I loved it, my time as a player on the LA Lasers women's team didn't last long after my run-in with the bottom of a player's cleats—those sharp spikes that grip the field. I could've left my short-lived football career in the hospital ER room. Yet something drew me back to the field. I had a choice to make. Give up on my dream of being a part of women's football? Leave the field disappointed? Or stay and find a different role to play?

I stuck around and became the team's general manager. Even though I'd never made a professional football game happen before, I loved producing and was a good organizer and motivator. With time, I adapted my organizational and interpersonal skills to handle the needs of the football team. I gained a new set of skills and gave the team a better alignment. In other words, when I was in a position to use my best skills, I blossomed, and the team shined.

In this chapter, you will learn about football player positions—who stands where and does what. I encourage you to use this chapter as an opportunity to reflect on the positions you assume in your own life. How do you feel in those positions? Empowered? Energetic? Do they serve you well? Do you operate at your peak? Can you push past obstacles towards your goal? Do you see your future potential? Or are you angry doing work you don't want to be doing? Does the work limit you, minimize either your skills or how you feel about the way you're using your talents?

Life is definitely a journey on which you'll hold a variety of positions. Will you shine? Or will you grind your way through? Remember, shining isn't about a spotlight hitting *you*. It's about something inside you coming alive and freeing your spirit to soar. When you shine, you align with your true self and have more peak experiences.

As Maslow says, "One's only rival is one's own possibilities. One's only failure is failing to live up to one's own possibilities." When you're in a position to do what you love, do what you were meant to do, put forward the uniqueness that is you, you feel unstoppable. It puts you in a kick-ass frame of mind, and you shine. You may have to immerse yourself to find that new position and tweak the position at times. Not so the sun hits your face, but so the light inside you can brighten the world.

Xs and Os

Introducing... Xs and Os. No, that doesn't mean hugs and kisses. In football, when coaches draw a football plan on paper, a whiteboard or a tablet, they use Xs and Os to indicate where players should line up for a play. On paper as in checkers, where your pieces are either red or black, a football player is either an X or an O. Easy to guess which side is represented by the Os—O is for offense. Now cross your forearms together in front of your chest and say, "You're not getting past me. Not on my watch." That's the defense—the Xs.

For the most part, Xs (the defense) defend their territory and their end zone, while the Os (offense) barrel downfield with the ball in hopes of entering the end zone the Xs are defending. Of the 46 players suited up to play, only eleven players from each team can be on the field at one time. That's 11 Xs and 11 Os. When they do take to the field, players fill specific positions and are tasked to use their skills as the team most needs them to. As team members, that's how players shine.

In this chapter, I want you to put your knowledge of Xs and Os to work by drawing their positions the way a coach would in a team meeting. You can start by placing the football itself on the chart, placing a tiny oval in the middle of the page. Then draw a single horizontal line through the football. This is the line of scrimmage, or LOS, and represents the current location of the football.

The line of scrimmage is an imaginary line that transects the field horizontally. Offense takes their position on one side of the line; their opponent's defense on the other side, O player facing X player. Although the line of scrimmage is represented as a straight line in drawings, the location of the football establishes a *neutral zone*, about the length of the ball, between the two teams. Until a play begins, the neutral zone is off limits to all players except the person hiking the ball.

As I mentioned before, the offense always starts the action and the defense responds to what they see. Keep that in mind as you go through this introduction to players and positions.

The A-B-Cs of Offensive

With 46 players suited up on one team and 11 on the field for each play, you might be wanting to skip over this chapter, thinking it's going to be TMI—too much information. Now you have to think about Xs and Os. Oh my. What's next—ABCs? Trying to follow all the players running around on the field may prompt you to get up and leave the room. "More snacks, anyone?" "Who wants another beer?"

I beg you—don't leave the room. Not yet. Stay. I promise I'm going to make this simple. I haven't forgotten that this book is meant as a primer, to get you going. It's not an encyclopedia. So I'm not going to tell you every detail of every position but just enough to follow the action.

To make it super easy to remember, I'll break down the offensive positions into three simple categories. It's going to be *so* easy, you'll wonder why no one ever put it in these terms before. Well, sometimes it's easier for a woman than a man (like the Green Bay fan I met in the elevator) to break down the game into its simplest form. Coach "D" at your service.

Are you ready? Let's go.

Throughout most of the game, there are three categories of offensive players on the field. I'm going to call them the A–B–Cs of offense. There might be exceptions for special plays, as when a team kicks the ball to start the game or tries for extra points. But for the most part, there are three categories: A–B–C. Okay, that's it. You're done. Only three categories of players you have to think about.

A — Agent
B — Blockers
C — Carriers

Let's take a closer look at the ABCs of offense.

A = The Agent

Agile and adaptable. Strong and ready. Plan in hand. That's the Agent of the offense—the quarterback. If you see the word "agent" and think of your favorite James Bond, Mission Impossible or Laura Croft movie, that's perfect. The quarterback is the football equivalent of the action agent who has the knowledge and skills to put an intricate plan into action or make something up when the plan goes wrong. The quarterback says, "Go," and when and where.

As the agent, the quarterback ignites the action of just about every play during a football game. If there's an exception, it's probably a trick play to throw off the expectations of the defense. So, if there's one position you want to keep your eyes on while learning about the players, it's the quarterback. No surprise that quarterbacks are often elected or chosen captains of their team.

A football play begins when the person in front of the quarterback, a player called the *center*, hikes or *snaps* the ball to the quarterback. This move is the "between your legs" move that always looks pretty personal. But it's just how every play begins. In chapter 7, I share some fun history of how snapping the ball evolved. What the quarterback does with the ball once he gets it— gives it to a runner, throws it to a receiver, or runs with it himself—is determined by the directions the coach gives the quarterback before the play begins and also how the defense responds. You'll learn about specific offensive plays in chapter 7.

To place your first two players on the chart, draw a circle beneath the football. Drop down a bit and draw another circle. Make the lower circle a little bigger so you can find it more easily.

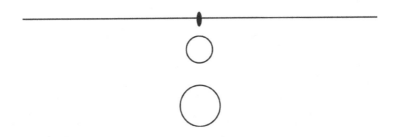

Inside the top circle, write the letter C for center. This is the player who hikes the ball to the quarterback. Inside the bottom larger circle, write the letters QB for quarterback.

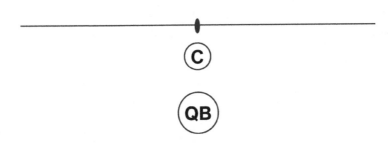

The Agent is now safely in place.

Let's bring on the Bs.

B = Blockers

"Refrigerator." That's what teammates called William Perry, one of the biggest, baddest blockers in the NFL. Weighing in "a biscuit shy" of 350, he was so big that when his team won a Super Bowl, his size-25 championship ring became the largest in NFL history. While William the Refrigerator actually played defense, his size and stature is an excellent example of the "B" category of offensive players—the Blockers.

It's true that players in the B category can often pass for highway support columns. If you imagine four or five such columns stacked in a row, you start to get a feeling for what blockers create—a strong, impenetrable wall referred to as the "front line." That wall has to be impenetrable because one of their primary roles is to defend and protect their quarterback, the agent of action, who is vulnerable to getting hit from all sides.

The other role of the offensive line is to open up gaps for runners to slip through. Working in tandem, they act like a two-ton wrecking ball. Wherever they swing their weight, something's gotta give and open up. If the quarterback hands the ball to a runner, then the front line of blockers gangs up and leans left or right to create a gap for the runner to get through.

Before you draw O positions for the blockers, draw a rectangular box just below the line of scrimmage. This represents the power wall blockers create as a single unit front line. And yes, the Center, after hiking the ball, becomes part of that mighty offensive front line.

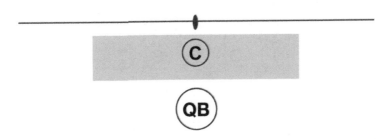

From a life perspective, this is where you "hold the line." Where you keep defensive forces from interrupting your own personal efforts of moving forward on your goals. This is where you take a stand for what you want.

Now add two circles to the left of the center and two circles to the right to represent the individual blockers on the front line. Fill in each new circle with a B. To keep things simple with the ABCs of offense, I could just leave it there. You can just think of this as a wall as "blockers" and move on.

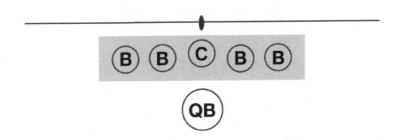

If, however, you're curious about these actual position names, sharpen your pencil and lean in. There are two offensive guards, one to the left and right of the center. Guards do just what their name suggests—they guard and protect the quarterback. Next to each guard is an offensive tackle. Tackles try to open up the line so whoever is carrying the ball can wiggle through. Although you'll see other players line up on either end of this block of players, the two guards, two tackles and center make up the core of the offensive front line.

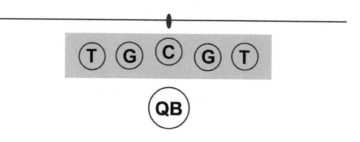

C = Carriers

"C" is for Carriers. There are two types of carriers—those who are handed the ball and those who are thrown the ball. The carriers who are handed the ball line up behind the quarterback and the front line of blockers. Their official title is "running back," so add two circles beneath the QB and write an R in each circle.

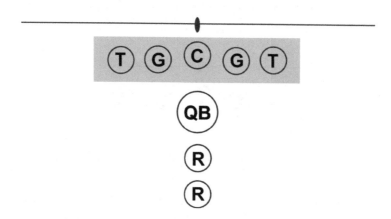

In general, running backs start behind the quarterback, either in a straight line or one on either side, and run forward past the line of scrimmage to advance the ball forward. Sometimes their gains are small. But in football, as in life, every yard forward counts! The various ways players line up are called formations. When running backs fall in line behind the quarterback, as in the image above, it's referred to as an "I" formation.

Running backs don't just run—they push, plow, and steamroll their way through a stack of players to gain a few precious yards. At the same time, they need to be fast enough so when a hole in the man-made wall is created, they can break free and fly down the field. Good running backs need balance to remain standing no matter what hits them, as well as good X-ray vision to see where an opening in the line might occur. They have to be strong *and* agile.

Speaking of strong and agile, there are two types of running backs—fullbacks and halfbacks. Halfbacks are agile, fast runners and tend to be the principal ball carrier, whereas the strong, hefty fullback blocks, protects or clears a path for the halfback. Sometimes this group—quarterback, fullback, halfback—is referred to simply as the *backs*.

The other type of carrier requires the player to catch and *then* carry the ball. These carriers are called wide receivers. As opposed to a blocker's beefy, boxy build, or the lighter, compact physique of a running back, wide receivers are typically tall, lean and strong. Many appear statuesque and make some of the most dramatic plays in football. When some receivers jump up to catch the football, I'm reminded of the famous ballet dancer Mikhail Baryshnikov, who could clear almost six feet when he leaped in the air. Football as ballet? Hey, I'm looking at football as life, so why not?

If you were a wide receiver, where would you line up? The best chance to break away from the crowd and catch the ball is, of course, to line up on an outer end of the line of scrimmage away from the hefty front-line traffic.

Before we pencil in the wide receivers, there's one more player that makes up the 11-person offense—the tight end, represented by the TE circle in the image below. Tight ends are hybrid players—think B + C position. They line up to the right of the offensive line, so they can help block. But they are also eligible to receive the ball, too.

Depending on the play, there are various ways offensive players can line up in formation. Here is one example.

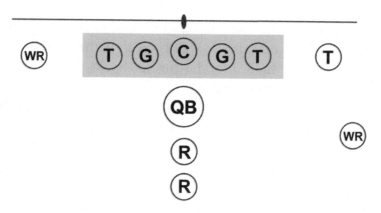

The offensive team must have at least seven players on the line of scrimmage at the start of every play. Blockers make up five. Only the outer two players on the line of scrimmage are eligible to catch the ball. That's why you'll often see the second wide receiver drop back behind the tight end. Although any offensive player can run with the ball, only the backs and receivers are eligible to catch a forward pass.

Although it takes skill to play any of these football positions, wide receivers, running backs and quarterbacks are referred to as *skilled players* on the team as they are the ones who would most likely handle the ball and score. Don't forget—you are the one who handles the ball for your team. You're the one who will score. So, keep thinking of ways to become a more skillful player in whatever you choose to do.

As you'll learn in the next chapter, a team can get penalized if play begins with more than 11 players on the field or more than seven players on the offensive line. Here's a head count of the players that make up the 11-member offense.

> A = 1 agent (quarterback)
> B = 5 blockers (one center, two guards, two tackles)
> C = 4 carriers (two running backs, two wide receivers)
> B + C = 1 blocker/carrier (one tight end)

And a partridge in a pear tree.

The Big "D" — Defense

I've identified the offense positions as A-B-C. I can keep the groupings of player positions simple and add "D" for Defense. Across the line of scrimmage are the defensive linemen, often referred to as the "D" line. Rather than blocking incoming traffic the way the offensive line does, the D line players actually *are* the traffic.

In the Xs and Os layout, note the defensive positions are placed inside a box with a gray X behind it. Find the two defensive tackles and two defensive ends on the front defensive line. Defensive tackles rush in to tackle offensive running backs carrying the ball. Defensive ends have some flexibility to follow a runner, a receiver, or even rush in to tackle or *sack* a quarterback.

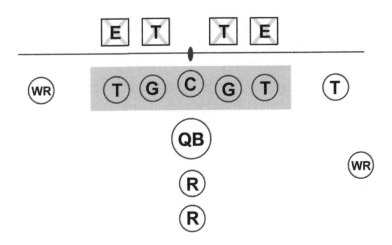

What if an offensive running back, or even the quarterback, powers through the D line? No worries. A few steps back are three defensive linebackers. They plug the gaps and guard against the break-through run—either from the quarterback or one of the offensive running backs. Think of it this way—the line*backers* back up the linemen.

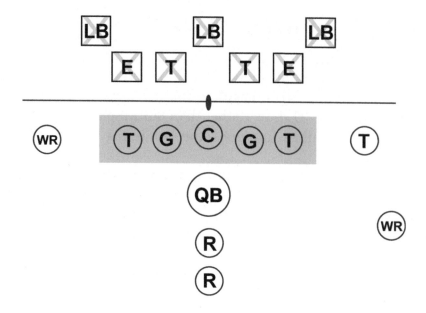

The remaining defensive players are the defensive backs and they provide a secondary line of defense. They include two cornerbacks and two safeties.

Cornerbacks line up just behind the linebackers toward the two corners of the playing area. Their job is to keep the wide receiver from catching a pass downfield or to tackle him the moment he does. When a cornerback leaps higher than the receiver and catches the ball, that team gets possession of the ball and their offense takes the field.

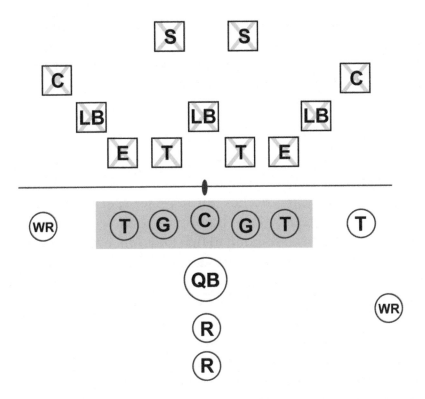

There's a wonderful line from an old Frank and Ernest comic strip by Bob Thayer. Referring to the dancer Fred Astaire, the words go, "Sure, he was great, but don't forget that Ginger Rogers did everything he did, backwards...and in high heels." In football, Fred Astaire is the wide receiver prancing down the field in hopes of leaping up to catch the ball. Ginger Rogers is the defensive corner who follows his lead, oftentimes moving backwards, sideways or both at the same time.

To provide a safety net in case a runner or receiver breaks through the line and heads for the end zone, there are two safeties in the backfield. From that perspective, the safeties can see how and where the action is unfolding, then go there to shut down the play. Both safeties and cornerbacks are considered defensive skill positions.

These are the basics of a football team's defensive player lineup. Is there more to know? There's always more to know about any aspect of football! I'm hoping this sketch of the positions helps you get your head in the game and *want* to learn more.

Special Teams and Kickers

Throughout a game, teams have to perform certain tasks, such as kicking the ball, which fall outside basic offense-defense maneuvers. For this, coaches put together special teams. There are four special teams. Two (on offense) handle kicking the ball and two (on defense) respond to that kick. Once again, the mirror concept is at play. Offense acts, defense reacts. Of the two kicks, one sends the ball downfield, either by kicking or punting it, and the other is an attempt to score points. You'll learn more about scoring points in chapter 6.

There are two kicking player positions—a kicker and a punter. The kicker uses a "free kick" approach to kick the ball downfield. In a free kick, the kicker either sets the ball on a small plastic tee or has another member of the special team hold the ball in place. The kicker then "freely" runs up to the stationary ball and kicks it. A free kick is used to kick off a game, to change possession after a team scores, and to score extra points.

The punter doesn't have the same luxury as the free kicker because, when a punter kicks, the ball never sits still or touches the field. Instead, a center-like player called the *long snapper* hikes the ball directly to the punter who stands about 15 yards back. The punter catches the ball and performs a drop kick—where he drops the ball in front of his foot and kicks it. The moment the long snapper hikes the ball, the football is live, and the defense special team can rush in to block the punt and tackle the punter. So, the punter has to kick the ball as far away as possible as quickly as possible.

You'll find other unique players on a special teams unit. For example, the receiving team will have a super-fast return runner who catches the ball, then runs like the wind downfield before getting tackled. Or defensive linemen who can leap up high enough to block a kick.

Special team players are a good example of the Shine principle. They drill and practice their skills to achieve a highly focused result. And when they perform at their peak, they shine.

When life demands a little something extra from you, remember that you, too, have special skills. When you take the time to identify and hone those skills, you can tackle gritty problems outside your normal routine the way a football player on a special team does.

Player Numbers

One aid to identifying player positions is the gigantic 8-inch-high number on the back of each football jersey. While a number can't be chosen arbitrarily, players do have some options within a designated range of numbers dedicated to the position they're playing. When primary numbers are already being used for a position, a player can choose from assigned alternative numbers.

PLAYER POSITIONS	PRIMARY NUMBERS	ALTERNATE NUMBERS
Quarterbacks, Punters, Kickers	1-19	
Running Backs	20-49	
Centers	50-59	60-79
Offensive Linemen	50-79	
Defensive Linemen	50-79	90-99
Wide Receivers	80-89	10-19
Tight Ends	80-89	40-49
Defensive Linebackers	50-59	90-99
Cornerbacks & Safeties	20-49	

The Coaching Staff

If you hear someone at a football game or practice say—"Hey, Coach, how's it going?"—you might see a dozen people turn their heads. While each NFL team has a Head Coach, there may be as many as 15 assistant coaches who play a role in supporting the team's goals. Let's start at the top with the head coach.

Remember the three-legged stool? The role of a head coach is basically what you do when you take the observer role in life. You know what you want, what your goal is. You have to figure out the best way to reach that goal given the resources you have in your personal toolkit and the obstacles facing you.

Each week of the football season, and months leading into it, the head coach determines what's not working, or who's not working in which positions, then revises the team strategy and plan of attack. What might have been a good defense for last week's game may not be the best approach for next week's game. With the input of the entire coaching staff, and after watching hours of game recordings, changes are made and a revised plan is implemented.

While an NFL head coach may develop an overall game strategy and plan, assistant coaches take on the task of drilling specific plays. The job of choosing the right offensive play during a game typically falls to the offensive coordinator. Another assistant coach might be assigned to follow the actions of the quarterback, since the success of any game relies heavily on the quarterback's performance. The quarterback coach monitors everything from footwork to throwing technique and even monitors a quarterback's overall mental and physical state. For the defense, there's the defensive coordinator who develops and oversees the defense's game plan.

At the end of the game, when a sideline reporter holds out her microphone to get a comment, it's usually to the head coach—to hear about the strategy they came into the game with, how they feel their team performed and what they'll now work on to improve.

Taking care of the players' bumps, bangs and bruises are the trainers. I've gotten my share of bruises just throwing and catching the football. Those pointy ends can sting! But bigger injuries need serious attention. Trainers help bridge the gap between the medical advisor's evaluation and supporting the player to get back into the game as soon as possible.

GMs and Owners

If the head coach is all that, who hires the head coach? That would be the general manager, or GM. During televised games, you often see a shot of a small group of people in the VIP box. That's where the GM, family members and team owners hang out. While not owning the football team, the GM has the responsibility of pulling it all together as a successful business. And the investment in an NFL football team is over one billion dollars. To think that a century ago when the NFL started, the price of a team franchise was $100!

A football GM manages the football team and support staff. If a change needs to be made, it's the GM who will oversee the firing, hiring and contract negotiations. A lot of head coaches like to have a hand in the player selection process, since they're the ones who have to make the selection of players work. For this reason, some coaches are both head coach and GM. As Bill Parcels, past head coach of the New England Patriots, once said, "[If] They want you to cook the dinner, at least they should let you shop for the groceries."

For love of the game and/or money, owners pass down ownership of the team to family members as part of a trust or legacy. Even some coaches keep it all in the family. Mike Shanahan, who coached John Elway and led the Denver Broncos to two consecutive Super Bowl victories in the 80s, shared the same coaching honor with his son, Kyle Shanahan, head coach of the San Francisco 49ers. And John Elway, who played quarterback as a Denver Bronco for Mike Shanahan, became GM and President of the Denver Broncos.

Huddle Up

Some positions in life, like NFL team ownership, may be handed down to you. Others, like player positions, require an audition or tryout. Sometimes, you can use skills you already have. Other times, you may have to tweak your skill set or develop a new one. Improving at any position requires practice and patience. Yet the results can be rewarding.

Earlier in this book, I talked about having to give up playing on my WPFL team when I was injured. Toward the end of our season, after my stitches healed, the team needed someone to step into the defensive end (DE) position, which I'd never played. I missed being a player on the field and decided to give it a try. What a gift that turned out to be. By immersing myself in that position, I learned some subtleties of defense. In that role, I could go after someone, interfere with their plan, interject myself in the play, and reach up and grab the ball for my team. I had no idea how fearless I would be in that position. But I was, and it felt great! It made me feel powerful.

Joseph Campbell, an American author and professor, said, "The privilege of a lifetime is being who you are." As you apply the LIPSTICK Football principles, be on the lookout for positions or situations where you can operate at your best and feel those little life highs, or peak experiences, that put you in flow with the Universe. Remember, when you shine, you share the best of who you are with the world. Discover where you shine.

Break It Down

This chapter has covered football positions and the traits needed to excel in those positions. Get to know them and start to observe specific traits. Then think about your own skill set. What traits do you have that when exercised make you shine? What traits do you need to develop?

FOOTBALL

1. While watching a football game, find the middle of the line of scrimmage, where the ball is placed. Then find the center who hikes the ball to the quarterback to initiate play.

2. Watch the quarterback, who might be directly behind the center or a few yards behind. What does the quarterback do with the ball? Hand it to a runner or throw it to a receiver?

3. Where are the wide receivers lined up? Remember, they need a clear path to run downfield and catch the ball, so look on the outside edges of the lineup.

4. Is the defensive line trying to rush in and tackle the quarterback? What are the secondary defensive players doing? Following a receiver downfield?

5. As you're watching a game, grab paper and a pencil and draw Xs and Os where the players line up. It's fun to do and a great way to review.

6. After you've drawn the Xs and Os, erase one position at a time and replace it with the name of that position. Don't worry if you don't remember them all. Just learn a few at a time.

LIFE

1. Have you ever had a "peak experience" or been in a position that made you shine? What were you doing when you felt that "life high?" Write about it in your journal. Remember, what you focus on grows.

2. Is it possible to recreate or simulate those circumstances? Can you create another opportunity to shine? For example, I'll never march in the Longhorn band again, but playing music with others always makes me shine.

3. Are you drawn to a football position? If so, which one? Why? Understanding why you like a certain position or activity—

what specific aspects of it appeal to you—can be valuable as you define the position you want to play in your own life.

4. You have many skills and talents. Which ones make you shine? Make a list and keep it close.

5. If you're ever in a slump, or need a boost, look at your list and choose to do something you know will be fun and that will give you energy.

Chapter 6

TRACK

Rules of the Game

You can't manage what you don't monitor.

—Diana Weynand, Author/Coach

In chapter 4, I encouraged you to exercise the Play principle—to play and dream. Dreaming isn't just fun, it's essential before starting a journey. After all, except for the occasional wanderlust road trip, you wouldn't take a vacation without choosing a destination first. And a dream is just that—a destination. A destination of the heart.

Choosing a destination is sometimes the easiest part of a journey. Your heart says, "I've always wanted to see Paris." Great! To ride that dream into reality, you have to shift the reins from your heart to your head—from "I want this" to "Now how am I going to get it." You have to make a plan. Draw a map. Set some goals. Track your progress. Define the rules.

A human brain has a left and a right hemisphere, and each excels at different tasks. The right side is dreamy, creative and artistic. The left is analytical and methodical, you might even say goal-oriented. The left hemisphere of your brain controls muscles on the right side of your body, and the right controls muscles on the left. By working together, they integrate your actions. It's similar with dreams and goals. Dreams give goals their underlying meaning, while goals give dreams structure and put them on a path to fruition. Although dreams and goals are different, they must be aligned in purpose.

Before you put your dream on a path, you have to get out in front of it and scout the territory. Once you've surveyed the playing field, so to speak, you can set guidelines and deadlines for how and when you will reach your target destination. You say you've always wanted to see Paris? Okay. How will you get there? Where will you stay? When will you go? How long will you be there? What exactly do you want to see?

In this chapter, I'll cover the rules of a football game. Like goals, agreed-upon rules—whether for a vacation, a Zoom meeting, book club, or a football game—have value. They set clear expectations and define time parameters, boundaries, player positions and permissions. For example, if I'm on the field running with the ball, I need to trust that a defensive blocker won't grab the grill on my face mask and twist my head around like Linda Blair's in *The Exorcist*. When the whistle blows and the tackling starts, rules keep football safe and fair.

Does that mean the T Principle stands for tackle? It's a frequent occurrence in football and in life. When you tackle a goal and move forward on your project, you feel victorious for a bit...then carry on. If you *get* tackled or knocked down by one of life's defensive moves, you probably get back on your feet...and carry on.

But *how* will you carry on? Will anything be different? If getting blocked and tackled is a "one off" for you—something that just happens occasionally, that's great. If, however, you trip over the same barrier time and again, rerun plays and moves that don't work, or remain stuck in a repeating pattern with no end zone in sight—you need to do more than just carry on. You need to track.

Introducing the T Principle — TRACK

In pioneering days, a tracker would ride ahead of the traveling group to survey the best path forward. Regular roads might be blocked or washed out from a flood. Some mountain passes might be too treacherous. By exploring the possibilities, the tracker would map out the safest and most efficient route to the group's destination and then guide the group forward. Were it not for trackers, many more newcomers would have lost their lives tackling the wild frontier.

You are the tracker in your life. If you get thrown off course or if things don't go the way you planned, it does no good to blame the defense. Instead, you have to convert "tackling" experiences into meaningful change. To do that, you make a conscious effort to observe and learn from them.

Start by leaning into the third leg of your three-legged stool and call on your inner coach. And then do what Walt Whitman suggests, "Be curious. Not judgmental." Become Sherlock Holmes and draw upon your super-sleuth powers of detection. Or use the journalists' five Ws—who, what, where, when, and why—and throw in H for How. Analyze the "event"—either the big win or the thing that messed you up. Football coaches do it all the time. You can, too.

Asking questions is how you gather data. And if that sounds clinical, that's exactly what you want. Remember my UT Longhorn Band maestro, Mr. D? During our on-field rehearsals, he'd walk the sidelines watching us practice our half-time routine. Sometimes he'd go missing. Glancing around, I'd find Mr. D perched high in the stands getting a bird's eye view of his band in action.

From the stands, Mr. D could listen and watch our routine from the perspective of an audience member. Were we hitting our marks? When did we step out of line and why? How did we sound? Then he'd hike back down to the field and put us to work fixing those aspects of our performance.

Mr. D didn't climb the stadium steps for his health. I'm sure that was good exercise for him, and he did live to be 95. He climbed those steps for a "10,000-foot view" where he could track progress and reimagine ways we could be the stellar band our fans expected us to be. Like Mr. D, you have to get in front of your journey or climb to a "higher" perspective if you want to make substantive changes.

Of course, you can't start tracking until you put your dream into action. So, as you learn the rules of football in this chapter, get *out* of your warm-up outfit and into a uniform—it's kick-off time. Create a game plan, start your game clock and begin tracking your forward progress.

You are the coach, the maestro, the tracker. You are holding the ball. Will you get knocked down on the field of life? Will obstacles block you? Will you get pulled off course? Yes, but don't let that stop you. Tom Bodett, owner of the Motel 6 string of hotels, said, "In school, you're taught a lesson and then given a test. In life, you're given a test that teaches you a lesson."

After a win or after you get tackled, put on your coach's hat or tracker's gear, lean into that inquiring mode and ask, "What is life trying to teach me?" Answer that. Track progress on that. Apply it as you move to your next goal, and the next one. Tackle or be tackled. That part isn't so important. Just track because, and this is important, you can't manage what you don't monitor.

Rules of the Game

Can you name a sport that does *not* have a pretty hefty rule book? Probably not. If you could, it would be a sport where players get hurt more frequently and spend time arguing about who won the play. Or it might be street football, where the oldest young players make up the rules as they go along.

Rules provide clarity. When players know the rules that bind them in their positions, they can relax into the game. "I can tackle this way, but not that. I can line up here, but not there." With everyone on the same page, players can perform their jobs more confidently and coaches can track their team's progress more effectively.

Rules also establish standards and expectations. For example, two hours and fifteen minutes before kickoff, two NFL game officials inspect all the footballs that will be used during the game to make sure they meet the official size, weight and air pressure requirements. The balls are then given to the K-Ball Coordinator (KBC) who, acting like the football police, guards them until 10 minutes before the game and double checks their pressure throughout the game. With this attention to detail, players on both teams can trust the footballs will be the same throughout the game and also from game to game.

Not all of the current rules of football were in place when the game began over 100 years ago. Some rules have been changed and new ones added. If you learn the basic rules in this chapter, you can watch the game and know why attention is being paid to certain moves at certain times. If you want to take a deeper dive, read or download the 2021 NFL Rulebook or watch the NFL Video Rulebook.

Coin Toss and Kick Off

"Flip you for it?" Every NFL game begins with a kickoff from one team's defense to the other team's offense. But who decides which offense starts first? When I played street football with my brother and his friends, they'd flip a coin, call heads or tails, and let the coin toss winner pick up the ball. The players took their places and our scruffy street football game would begin.

It's not all that different in an NFL game. In fact, when the coin toss was first used in American football back in 1892, the players themselves handled the toss, just as my brother did. It wasn't until 1921 that the head official (the referee) tossed the coin. The purpose of the coin toss, however, has remained the same—to determine who gets the ball first and which side of the field each team takes to start the game.

Here's how it works. Three minutes before the scheduled start of an NFL game, at the 50-yard line in the middle of the field, game officials meet with three captains from each team—usually the quarterback and two other players. The referee flips the coin. A captain from the visiting team calls heads or tails. The coin lands and the coin-toss winner chooses one of the following:

1) Kick or receive the ball (start as defense or offense).

2) Pick which side of the field to start on.

3) Defer the choice to the second half.

There are strategies and advantages to picking one option over another. Receiving the ball at the beginning of the game gives a team's offense the chance to score early. Deferring to receive the ball at the second half kickoff, a relatively new and popular option added in 2008, gives a team more ball time when they might need it most—coming down the home stretch of a game.

Choosing a side of the field is sometimes called "choosing wind." Wind, weather, sun, lights, time of day, and time of year may not always affect the game but can sure affect individual players. A heavy wind can reduce how far a quarterback throws the ball and limit how far a punter can kick. Facing a glaring afternoon sun makes it difficult for receivers to see the ball as it comes hurtling down on them. Still, whatever the impact of bad weather, it doesn't impact a team for the entire game, because field position is switched every quarter.

No matter what choice is made and by whom, fair is fair and football rules are balanced. If the coin-toss winner chooses to receive the ball at the start of the game, the coin-toss loser gets to pick the side of the field they want to start on. If the coin-toss winner chooses to defer their choice to the second half, the coin-toss loser gets to choose how they want to start the game—to kick, receive, or choose a field side.

To kick off a game, the ball is placed on a tee at the 35-yard line of the kicking team. Ten players of the kicking team—five on one side of the ball and five on the other—line up no more than one yard behind the ball. The kicker drops back and kicks. And official play begins.

Downs and Forward Progress

1st and ten.
2nd and six.
3rd and three.
4th and one.
No, this isn't a "Who's on first" joke. The numbers above spell momentum. When you get to know the game, they will make you feel something about what's happening in that moment. Is your team in trouble? Is it do-or-die time? Or are they sitting pretty? Let's break it down so you know when you should get excited, sit on the edge of your seat in anxious anticipation, or refresh your drink.

Whenever the offense gets possession of the football, they have four tries to move the ball 10 yards. Each try or attempt is called a down. The term "down" actually refers to setting the ball down on the ground in between plays, which was a departure from football's parent sport, soccer, where the ball moves freely between teams and rarely stops. In today's football, the ball is placed or set down where the offense's forward progress stopped. (You can read more about the evolution of downs in chapter 8.)

You might think moving the ball ten yards in four downs is no biggie. If you paced out the field in chapter 4, you may have conquered 10 yards with ten long strides in a few seconds. Now, in your mind's eye, place five 200- to 250-pound-plus, rippling-muscled players in front of you. When you're staring down a 1,000-pound human wall, it's a different story. The reward for going ten yards? You are given another four chances, or downs, to move the ball another 10 yards.

Each down begins pretty much the same way. The center hikes the ball to the quarterback, who typically hands it off to a running back or passes it to a receiver. When an opponent tackles the runner or receiver and stops forward progress of the ball, the head official whistles to end action. The game clock is stopped, and the offense regroups to prepare a play for the next down. One of the statistics the NFL tracks is how many third-down conversions a team has. That's the number of times a team was able to go 10 yards in just three downs.

The beauty of the down system, beyond getting to stop and regroup, is forward progress. Forward progress is an interesting concept in football and in life. You know the old saying: two steps forward, one step back? Let's say a player carries the ball forward 10 yards but is pushed back three yards before the official whistles to end the play. Is the ball marked at that 10-yard gain? Or the net 7-yard gain where the player was finally brought down? In football, the offense gets to keep every one of those sweet, precious ten yards that represent the furthest point in the player's forward progress.

Thinking about the down system may provide an effective way for you to break up your long trek to the end zone into smaller segments. And don't forget to acknowledge the forward progress you make along your journey. Every step or yard is a win you can claim—just like a football team's offense gets to do.

Virtual Markings

The more ways you can observe and take stock of your forward progress on the field and in life, the better you can manage and control your journey. You know, of course, about the white painted lines and hash marks up and down a football field. Those are permanent. In 1998, through the magic of broadcast technology, the visionary company SportsMEDIA Technology

(SMT) brought tracking yardage to a whole new level by creating virtual lines.

SportsMEDIA Technology (SMT) virtual line system

None of the virtual lines are white, so it's easy to distinguish them from the painted field markings. Instead, you will see a yellow first down target line, a blue line marking the line of scrimmage, and at times a red line marking the 20-yard line at the beginning of the red zone. If a field goal is an option, there might be a virtual line to indicate where the ball needs to be for a potentially successful kick. Before the ball is snapped, you might see a "down and distance" marker. All this virtual information moves in tandem with the offense to track forward progress with the ball.

Because of my background in video, I enjoy the technical process behind virtual marking. (Check out my book *How Video Works*.) If you're a tech geek like me, you might enjoy reading more about virtual field markings. If electronics don't interest you, no worries. Just know that the colorful virtual lines are there to help you track your team's progress more easily. (For more ways to monitor a team's progress on the field, watch SMT's Highlight Reel at the bottom of their Home page. You can find their link in the Acknowledgements.)

The Chain Crew

Jokester: How many people does it take to track 10 yards on a football field?

Answer: Three. No, really. Three.

Introducing... the chain crew, sometimes referred to as the chain gang. This team of three is part of the officiating team, and it tracks the offense's forward progress—down by down, yard by yard. Each crew member carries a big stick. Haha. Two of the sticks or poles have orange and black circles, like rings of a target. The third pole has a box that displays a large number, indicating the number of the current down—1, 2, 3 or 4.

The chain crew stands about six feet off the sideline toward the back of the restricted zone. Remember, the restricted zone is reserved for active players completing a play and for officials who monitor action along the sideline. The two poles with the black and orange bull's-eye target at the top are connected by a 10-yard chain. One pole is planted at the first down location while the second is set ten yards forward as the target destination. The pole with the number box tracks forward progress. Wherever the ball is placed for the current down, the number pole lines up with it and the number is changed to reflect the next down.

When it's a super close call and the ball may not have progressed the full ten yards, an official will call the chain crew out to the field to measure the distance against the chains. You might even see the official hold up the part of the chain that represents the distance the ball has come short of the ten-yard target. You may also hear "Move the chains." If it's your team, that's a good thing. It means the offense reached their goal of 10 yards and they get another set of four downs.

Want to have some fun and meet two (fictional) yard markers? The Progressive Insurance company recently produced ads introducing viewers to Mark and Marcus. (View them at (www.LipstickFootball.com/extras.) The ads drive home the point that the target markers are bound together by a 10-yard chain, which is fine on a playing field but not as convenient in the real world. Which brings up the question—who's keeping track of your forward progress, and how?

Touchdown!

Getting the football into the end zone makes for some of the most studied and reviewed plays of all time, and it's where certain football rules come into sharp focus. There are two ways the offense can score a touchdown and earn six points. They can run the ball across the goal line, or throw the ball to a receiver who takes it into the end zone (or catches it there). To score, the offense may have to try both options over the course of a few downs.

Let's start with Option #1—running for a touchdown. Remember, the goal line represents an imaginary plane rising from the ground from one side of the field to the other. You might see a running back with outstretched arms literally leaping over a pile of players. All that's required to score is to pierce that invisible wall with the tip of the ball. Also, when a ball carrier touches the ball to one of the orange pylons on either end of the goal line—touchdown!

Option #2—passing to a receiver. Typically, a receiver runs down a sideline. For a "legal" catch, the receiver has to catch and secure the ball while keeping both feet, or toes, inside the end zone—before stepping or getting pushed out of bounds. You'll often see an official stop the game for a video review to make sure the catch was legal. On occasion, you might see a receiver catch a pass just inside the goal line, then dive across the goal line or touch a pylon to score a touchdown.

To win a game, players might have to cross a goal line several times using various plays. Tracking how you get into the end zone will boost your confidence moving forward and improve your game.

Extra Points

After making a touchdown, a team earns the right to make an extra point or two. The easiest way to earn an extra point is by kicking the ball over the goal post from the 15-yard line. This requires bringing the extra-point special team out to the field. If the kicker kicks the ball over the upright "U," between the two vertical posts, one point is added to the scoreboard. This free-kick approach to making an extra point isn't too risky and the success rate is around 94%.

The other option, a two-point conversion, is a riskier move, but earns a team two points on top of the six points for a touchdown. The "going for two" option places the ball at the opponent's 2-yard line. All the defensive players gang up on the other side of the LOS ready to block any move. That move could be a running back hurdling over the goal line, a wide receiver waiting to catch the ball on the other side of the goal line, or a quarterback sneak where the quarterback tricks everyone by leaping across the goal—ball in hand.

You wouldn't typically see a coach choose a two-point conversion in the first half of the game. So, when would you see it? That play is usually saved for later in the second half when those two points could win or tie the game. Compared to the high success rate of kicking an extra point, the success rate for two-point conversions is only around 49%. Sometimes the gamble works and sometimes it doesn't.

There's another way a team can make extra points. This time it's the defense who scores. Let's say the offense has the ball on their own two-yard line, which means they have to go 98 yards for a touchdown. Ouch. That's an uphill battle that requires steady focus and determination. If the offense starts a play at that 2-yard line, and the defense tackles the ball carrier behind the goal line, a *safety* is called, and the defensive team earns two points.

Field Goals and Punts

There are two additional kicks you'll see during a game—a field goal and a punt. One gets you points and the other gets you out of trouble. First, let's make points with a field goal.

A field goal looks like the extra-point free kick a team earns with a touchdown. It, too, uses special team players. There are two important differences, however. A field goal adds three points to the scoreboard, not one. And you typically see a field goal on a 4th down—when the offense is close to the end zone but probably can't get there in one try. A successful field goal can win a game or raise a team's score before players break for halftime. When it's not successful, possession changes hands at the line of scrimmage.

Field goals are a calculated risk—a matter of distance and ability. I recently saw Seattle Seahawks' Jason Myers kick a 61-yard field goal. That was fun, because the longest field goal in NFL history was a 64-yard field goal. How do you measure the distance of a field goal attempt? Let's say the ball is on the 20-yard line. It has to sail over the goal post, which sits ten yards back from the goal line, that makes it a 30-yard distance. And the player who holds the ball for the kicker is positioned about eight yards back from the line of scrimmage. That's now a 38-yard field goal attempt.

The other type of kick, also a 4th-down option, is called a punt. A punt doesn't score points, but it can get a team out of trouble. Let's say it's 4th down and the offense is in the middle of the field. No one has a leg strong enough to kick a field goal from that distance. And the offense doesn't want to turn over the ball to their opponent at that location. Instead, they use their 4th down to punt the ball farther downfield, pushing back their opponent's starting position.

Sometimes a punt lands or bounces into the end zone before the receiving team can touch it or catch it—creating a touchback. If a touchback occurs, the officials place the ball on the 25-yard line of the receiving team to begin play. There are no points for a touchback.

The Officiating Team

If you're ever in doubt about who's got the final say on a 100-yard-long and 53-yard-wide football field, here's a clue. It isn't the offense, defense or even the coach. It's the officiating team, or the "Football Zebras," as they're sometimes called because of their black-and-white-striped shirts. It takes a team of seven officials to keep track of game time and monitor action across the field— side to side and end to end. Here's an overview of who does what, and where, to uphold the rules of a football game.

Referee (R)

Of the seven officials, only one wears a white baseball hat—the referee. As the lead official, the referee controls the game and has final authority on all decisions. Some of the referee's duties include officiating the coin flip and announcing penalties so the stadium and television audience can hear the call. The referee lines up on the right side of the quarterback behind the offensive players.

Umpire (U)

The official assigned to action at the line of scrimmage is the umpire. It might be helpful to think of a baseball umpire who stands just behind the catcher at home plate. A football umpire stands close to the line of scrimmage—about five yards back on the left side of the quarterback. From this perspective, the umpire can monitor specific actions.

For example, did the offense fumble the ball? Which team recovered it? Did a blocker hold on to another player? That's illegal. Did the quarterback release the ball from behind the LOS, or cross over and then throw it? Standing amidst the offensive players, the umpire is also in a position to do a quick head count before each play. There have to be seven offensive players on the line of scrimmage and there can be no more than 11 players from each team when play begins.

Down Judge (DJ)

Remember the chain crew that tracks downs and yardage? Those three report to the down judge who stands in the restricted zone just off the sideline at the line of scrimmage. At the end of each play, the down judge steps onto the field and literally puts a foot down to mark the forward progress of the ball.

Interestingly, the down judge position was originally referred to as the head linesman. In 2017, the NFL Head of Officiating, Al Riveron, saw a young woman in training wearing an official head linesman shirt. He decided all officiating positions should be gender neutral and changed the position to down judge. Go, Al!

Line Judge (LJ)

On the opposite side of the field to the down judge is the line judge. The line judge performs a function like the down judge's and, in professional and college football, has an auxiliary chain crew to track and display forward progress.

Side Judge (SJ)

Three additional judges cover the defensive backfield. Along the same sideline as the down judge, a side judge determines where a ball carrier runs out of bounds. The side judge also observes whether receivers have control of the ball and touch both feet to the field before stepping out of bounds.

Field Judge (FJ)

Across the field from the side judge is the field judge. The field judge has a good view of the play clock and can call a "delay of game" penalty if the 40-second timer expires before the offense starts a play. A field judge might be called on to rule on a touchdown and whether or not a field goal attempt successfully "split" the uprights.

Back Judge (BJ)

The back judge—in the middle of the field and toward the end zone—is the farthest away from the line of scrimmage. The back judge rules on ball placement or touchdowns after running backs break through with a long run. This judge might rule on pass interference, illegal blocks, and incomplete passes.

Football officials are trackers, as you're learning to be. They track the action of the game. They track the yardage of a player's forward motion, where the ball is at any given time, what mistakes the players make and whether or not they should be penalized for those errors. Remember, you can't manage what you don't monitor. The officials monitor the game and ensure the rules are followed by both the offense and defense—regardless of position. This keeps the game balanced, fair and safe for all the players.

To learn more about the NFL officiating team, check out the neatly designed color-coded interactive graphic of the NFL officials and their assigned positions. You can find it at: (https://operations.nfl.com/officiating/the-officials/officials-responsibilities-positions/).

Penalties and Consequences

While individual players are called out for specific transgressions, it's the entire team that suffers the consequences. Depending on the severity of the misstep, a team could be penalized anywhere from five to 15 yards and in some situations even more.

The five-yard penalties include stationary penalties that occur prior to the ball being snapped. There are penalties for moving or twitching (false start), having too many players on the field when the play begins, and lining up in the wrong place (illegal formation). You might wonder how an official is able to determine this. They simply look at the number on the back of a player's jersey. (See chapter 5 for player numbers.)

A misstep when the ball is in motion incurs a 10-yard penalty. For example, players can't trip other players or restrict others' movements by using their hands or arms. That's holding and is typically a 10-yard penalty.

The more serious the crime, the more yardage a team is penalized. When someone grabs a face mask grill, it forcibly twists a player's neck and often in the opposite direction the player is running. Grabbing a face mask is a 15-yard penalty and automatic first down.

Quarterbacks are particularly vulnerable. When they have both hands on the ball and are looking downfield, they can easily be blindsided. It's okay to tackle the quarterback, but not with unnecessary roughness. A 15-yard penalty is given for roughing the passer. In fact, you can't treat any opponent with unnecessary roughness. If you do, that's also a loss of 15 yards and an automatic first down. If an official observes what seems to be a flagrant action, the player can be disqualified.

Another big penalty is pass interference. If a receiver is running downfield and leaps up to catch a pass, a defensive player can't interfere with the process of the receiver catching the ball. The defensive player can get in between the ball and the receiver for an interception but cannot hold the receiver back from trying to catch it. Typically, with this penalty, the ball is placed at the site of the foul and there's an automatic first down.

Some of these rules have been around a while. For example, roughing the quarterback, a no-brainer, has been a rule since 1938. Others have been added to the rulebook more recently. In 2018, a new penalty was created to prohibit players from using their helmets to make direct contact against an opponent. No butting rams allowed.

Huddle Up

As you learn about the rules of football, remember they are there because players and coaches tracked action over time and determined there was a necessity for each and every one of them. So, as you track your own moves and progress, take a time-out now and then to really examine your steps. After all, NFL teams get three time-outs per half to regroup and consider their options or review their plays. Shouldn't you? There is great benefit of a "10,000 foot" view or perspective.

Break It Down

It's goal time. Time to get your dream up on its feet—to craft the best and smartest way to get it into the end zone so you can score. The sooner you define this process for your own goals and clarify your expectations, the sooner you'll be able to knock back obstacles stopping your forward progress and honor them as the life lessons they really are.

FOOTBALL

1. Watch a football game and look for the referee, the official with the white hat. Key into a few of the referee's duties, such as reviewing a play, announcing a penalty and conferring with the other officials.

2. Watch for penalties that occur before the ball is hiked. How many yards is the team penalized?

3. When you see a field goal attempt, calculate the actual distance of the kick, not just the yard line where the ball is located. (Spoiler alert, commentators often announce it.)

4. Watch a televised game and look for the virtual lines that mark the line of scrimmage (usually blue) and the 10-yard target line (yellow). Do you see any other virtual markings?

5. Want to learn more about the evolution of NFL rules? You can read about it at https://operations.nfl.com.

LIFE

1. Key into your own goals. Where are they on the playing field? Are they getting close to the end zone? Why, or why not? Track your efforts so you can monitor your forward progress.

2. Look closely at one of your wins and break it down. Knowing, and remembering, how you won will keep the "winning" feeling alive longer and encourage you to do it again.

3. When something doesn't go as planned, schedule a time-out for yourself to track what happened so you know how to do it better next time. Be curious, not judgmental.

4. If a football team gets another four downs by advancing 10 yards, what treat or reward can you give yourself if you reach a short-term goal? If you reach the end zone?

5. How will you hold yourself accountable if you don't make your 10-yard goal within the time limit you've set for yourself?

Chapter 7

INITIATE

Routing the Play

---

*You'll never plough a field
by turning it over in your mind.*

—Irish Proverb

---

ootball coaches implement a game plan—an overarching
vision with strategies that sustain the team throughout the
entire season. You did something similar when you plotted
a path to your dream in the previous chapter. In psychological
studies, that long-range plan is aimed toward a *distal* goal: "distal"
as in "distant." Distal goals are far away from where you are now.
That distance could be a reference to time—as in the three years
it may take you to finish a degree, or the entire football season it
may take for a coach to develop a winning team.

The best way to move toward your distal goal is to take small
bites out of that big plan. The change you would make with a "small
bite" would be called a *proximal* goal: "proximal" as in "proximity,"
nearness. In football, that might be executing a play during the
current game. In life, it might be passing a required course for your

degree. It's easier to believe you could reach a proximal goal even if you have to stretch yourself a bit to do it. The question is—which is the most important in pursuing your dream? Distal or proximal? A big plan or a small step?

Through various studies, psychologists have found that the type of goal that gives a person the best chance of completion is a proximal goal. Proximal goals not only improve learning and performance but also build belief in one's ability to succeed in specific situations, such as performing a task. Setting a long-distance goal is important, yet not as motivating because the success factor is spread out over a longer time.

What you want and need is more immediate feedback. That is, not by waiting until you arrive at the end of your journey but periodically along the way. A football team gets four downs to move the ball 10 yards. If the players can do that, they get another four downs. Getting that next first down is a proximal goal.

In the previous chapter, you made a plan to bring your dream to life. But there's a huge difference between implementing a long-range plan and initiating a short-range play. You wore a coach's hat to craft the plan. Now it's time to be a player—an offensive player. Is the coach on the field? No. You are. Is the defense in motion? No. Not until you make your move. You've got a dream in your heart, a game plan in your mind—and now you've got the ball in your hands. What are you going to do with it?

Introducing the second I Principle — INITIATE

When I developed courses and wrote how-to books for video editing, I observed "action hesitancy" up close and personal. The type of editing I taught was on highly complex, computer-based software applications such as Apple's Final Cut Pro, Adobe's Premiere, and AVID. My distal goal was for students to become confident editors using a particular editing software. However, when students looked at the editing application, their eyes glazed over. I could see them freeze as though thinking, "I'll never learn this program."

To unfreeze them and make that distal goal easier to achieve, I filled my book and course with hundreds of proximal goals—small editing operational hands-on exercises—such as how to import footage, how to mark the portion of a video you want to use, how to adjust or fade volume, how to add an effect, and so on. Reaching a variety of proximal goals led to achieving the distal goal—learning the editing software.

If you've got kids, you probably have the movie *Frozen* on your watch list. Good movie. I enjoy watching how the characters in the story get frozen—as in stuck—and how they break through their limiting beliefs. I'm interested because I can get stuck or frozen when I don't know what to do next or, the reverse, when I get overwhelmed by too many choices.

Sometimes you need a pass on *how* you take action and simply support yourself to *take* an action. To that point, I want to share a song from my personal music playlist, Oleta Adams singing "Get Here," written by Brenda Russell. I encourage you to stop reading, take a minute and find the song on YouTube.

Gushy love stuff aside, Oleta has one distal goal—get person A closer in proximity to person B. And she offers several proximal goals that could do the trick, some realistic and some less so—trailway, railway, a plane, a caravan, a sailboat, slide down a slope, take a carpet ride or just use your mind. In the end, she says it doesn't really matter how Person A gets to her [plan be damned], she just wants them to "get here" however they can.

Not every play in a football game is so pretty it warrants 100 replays on a big screen. Some plays, although well designed, turn out messy, unproductive or awkward. But making one play will lead to another potentially better play. And tracking your progress as you move downfield toward your goal will motivate you even more.

Getting to the second "I" Principle means it's *Go Time*. Time to act on your plan and start initiating plays. As the saying goes,

"A thousand-mile journey begins with a single step." This chapter will cover a variety of both offensive and defensive plays and how they are called into action during a football game.

Choosing which play you make or step you take toward your goal is up to you. By offering over a dozen ways to "Get Here," Oleta tells you everything you need to know about initiating action. Don't squander opportunities to take action on your goal. And don't worry as much about how as when—*now*.

Implementing a Game Plan

Before players report for their first practice, football coaches develop a game plan for the season. They choose various plays and strategies that make up their playbook. Some may be standard "tried and true" plays that have been in use for years. Others might be new, hybrid or experimental.

A coach's playbook for the season might contain over 1,000 plays. In preparing for a single game, the coaching staff will review the plays and pick what they feel is the best combination of running and passing plays to defeat their opponent. By game day, the coaching team has culled something like 100 throwing or passing plays and 15-20 running plays.

That collection of game plays is neatly organized and then laminated to create a play call sheet, a sort of cheat sheet coaches hold during the game for quick reference.

You've seen coaches on television scanning for possible plays to meet the moment. If you take a close look, you might even see the plays organized into types, such as run or pass plays, red zone, and so on. Some categories get very specific and list plays that might be used, for example, on 3rd down with two to seven yards to go.

Although a "play" sounds like a singular action, each play is really a combination of moves involving the 11 team players on the field. While players have to know who does what, they mainly have to learn their job—how far downfield to run before turning around to catch a pass, whether to turn left or right with the ball, who to block so the running back can bust through the defensive line. And of course, players have to remember the name of the play and its ultimate goal or purpose. By game day, coaches will have drilled players until they can perform the necessary plays without hesitation.

You won't always know what's going to be thrown at you on the field—in sports and in life. When you rehearse a variety of options, as a football team does, you can prepare yourself to initiate specific actions that meet the moment.

Football Plays

With over 1,000+ possible plays for the season and over 100 honed plays for the upcoming game, what specific play should a coach call? The simple answer is—it all depends. For example, is it 4th down with one yard to go? If you're close to making a touchdown, you might try to run for that one priceless yard. If you're pushed back close to your own goal line, you'll want to punt the ball downfield as far away as possible. How much time is left on the game clock? Running plays take more time so, when you're ahead, "running out the clock" is a good plan. Or are you behind and need to grab as many yards as possible in the shortest amount of time? That might call for a passing play. Each play is designed as a tactical maneuver for a specific scenario during a game.

Can the defense have a play list, even though they don't carry the ball? You bet they can. And they do! A team's defense watches video of their opponent and designs ways to block what they anticipate will be their opponent's "go-to" plays. The defense will also initiate plays designed to intercept the ball or force a fumble. And don't forget the defense special teams brought in at various times: for example, to block a field-goal kick.

The more football you watch, the more familiar you'll become with types of plays. You'll even start to recognize them by name. Before I begin defining specific plays, let's go over how the play is delivered to the field during the game.

Initiating the Play

Tick tock. Tick tock. A team's offense has 40 seconds after the end of one play to decide on *and* initiate the next play. When a team isn't able to snap the ball before the 40-second clock hits zero, game play is stopped and the field judge calls a five-yard "delay of game" penalty. The line of scrimmage is moved back five yards and the offense has to repeat the down. As a game clock gets close to zero, the quarterback might call a time-out. That stops the clock and gives the team a chance to reset and try again.

Although quarterbacks lead the team's offense on the field, they don't usually call the plays. That's the job of the offensive coordinator, who sends a play to the field via the audio communication system in the quarterback's helmet. Sometimes the coordinator uses an assistant coach to actually do the communicating. You may have seen a QB raise his hand to cover the helmet ear hole, shutting out stadium noise. The coach is literally talking in the quarterback's ear. Coaches get only 25 seconds to communicate the play before the NFL uses a cut-off device to kill that communication.

The terminology quarterbacks use to initiate action and snap or hike the ball has a long and interesting history. Up until the 1890-1891 season, football great John Heisman of Heisman Trophy fame had been using the standard quarterback routine to initiate a play, which was to scratch the center's leg. When a false scratch on the opponent's team threw off his own team, he started using the verbal "Hike," which was crisp, short and easy to understand. After some time, the term "Hut" started being used. "Hut" could have come from the military "Atten-hut," also a short, crisp sound.

Of course, quarterbacks don't just walk up to the line of scrimmage and say, "Hut." They precede that with a few other words—a combination of colors and numbers to communicate an adjustment to the play, sometimes based on how they see the defense lining up. With this more complex messaging, today's football code to initiate action is referred to more broadly as an "audible."

In a New York Times article, "Hut! Hut! Hut! What?", Bill Peddington talks about the evolution of the audible. He says, "Much of it is mumbo-jumbo, phony phrases meant to confuse the defense." To see what he means, check out a fun YouTube video on my website (Extras page). In the end, an audible—no matter the colors, numbers or words—gets the job done of initiating a play.

Running Plays

Hand off—and run for it! A running play is one of two primary categories of plays the offense uses to get the ball downfield. Basically, the quarterback hands off the football to a running back who rushes into the defensive line. Why this is called "rushing" I'll never know. Running backs may be fast and speedy in a flat-out run, but put the defensive line's wall of weight in front of them and they're lucky if they eke out three or four yards. But that may be all the offense needs to convert to another first down.

In truth, running plays are a perfect example of how to chip away at your goals—bit by bit, a few yards at a time—to make sure you reach your destination. When you're consistent, it wears down the defense—in life and on the field. "Fatigue the D!" is a cry I would expect to hear from the fans who understand that strategy. By the second half of the game, or at least by the fourth quarter, the fatigued defense has a much harder time keeping the persistent and now fired-up running backs from breaking through and gaining yardage.

Former NFL player Bucky Brooks has these apt words about what to expect from the running game: "Think of the running game like a boxer's jab. You're not throwing the jab to knock the opponent out; you're using it to set up the big right-hand shots that lead to knockdowns."

You don't have to know the intricacies of every running play to follow a game. But if you learn the following three plays, it will help you track the action.

Dive (or Blast)

Let's review the offensive lineup. The image shows the "I" formation you learned about in chapter 5 where the running backs are lined up behind the quarterback. A guard is on either side of the center and tackles are next to them. While guards need to stay in place to protect the quarterback, the tackles can adjust their position to push and open up a pocket allowing one of the running backs behind them to drive up the middle, or side, of the defensive line.

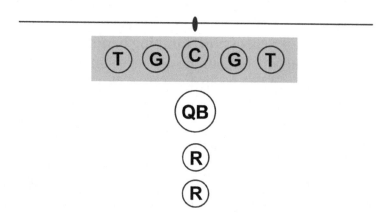

One of the simplest and most effective plays for breaking through the defensive line is called the *dive*. The offense uses this play to simply push through the defensive line and gain a yard or two to get a first down. Basically, the quarterback hands the ball to a running back. The offensive guard and tackle try to open up a hole for the running back to run through. When the defense sees who is running where, they close the gaps and try to block the runner. Force against force.

A similar play to the dive is the *blast*. This is a double-trouble play where two running backs work in tandem to blast through the front line. One running back acts as the lead blocker to open a lane and a second running back follows behind carrying the ball. Usually, the fullback is the lead blocker and the halfback is the ball carrier.

Counter

Counter to what you were expecting... in other words... this play is a fake. Not a fake play, but a play that fakes where the ball is going or may be going in order to throw off the defense. It's an intentional misdirection. Think of the previous play, the dive. It's simple and clean—a few mighty steps forward through the front line and you're done. The counter play has two steps. It will end up being a dive play, but it starts with a fake.

Step one: The quarterback turns right and fakes a handoff to a running back coming up on that side. But rather than deliver the ball, the quarterback turns left and...

Step two: The quarterback hands the ball off to the running back who then runs up the middle. Easy, right? It's the dive play but starting with a fake to confuse the defense.

A Draw Play

A third popular running play is the draw. This is another play where the quarterback fakes an action to start the play. To review, the dive play is a hand-off and straight run through the line. The counter play is that same run but preceded with a fake handoff to the opposite side.

The draw play shows a different kind of fake, with the quarterback dropping back as if to throw or pass the ball. Then he hands off to a running back who blasts through the defensive line. To remember "draw," you can think of the quarterback drawing out the defense and opening up a hole in the line for the running back to punch through.

If you want to "dive" into more running plays, check these out on Wikipedia.

Passing Plays

The other way the offense moves the ball downfield is when the quarterback passes it to a receiver. The handoff from the quarterback is not direct, as it is to a runner. Instead, in a passing play, the quarterback throws the ball to a rendezvous point. At the moment the quarterback releases the ball, no one is at that target destination. Within the few seconds it takes for the ball to arrive, a receiver runs to that destination and catches the ball. But in that time it's also possible for a defensive safety or cornerback to reach up and intercept the ball. With the ball moving freely in the air, passing can be riskier than running a play, but it can also result in a bigger yardage gain when the play is successful.

Although there is interplay between the quarterback and the receiver, they focus on two very different things. The receiver thinks about two Ds—distance and direction. How many yards (distance) downfield do I run before I make my move in a particular direction? The quarterback thinks about two Ts—time to target. How long do I wait before throwing the ball to allow the receiver time to reach the target?

Before getting into specific passing plays, let's review the receiver starting positions.

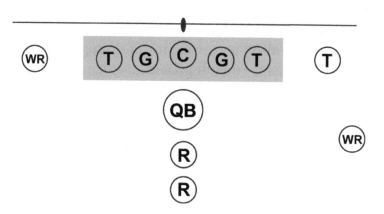

In the image, find the wide receiver who lines up far left on the line of scrimmage. Then find the other wide receiver on the opposite side a yard or so back from the line of scrimmage. The tight end, another eligible receiver, lines up to the right of the right tackle. Since there can be only two eligible receivers lining up on the LOS, that's often the tight end on the right, who can also serve as a front-line blocker, and the wide receiver on the left.

While a running play is an example of safely chipping away at your life goals, a passing play represents taking a risk. Will your effort pay off? Will the players and resources you need line up when and where you need them? Will you rendezvous with destiny and accomplish your goal? It may be risky, but when you "go for it" in life, as in football, you just might end up with a greater gain. And you'll never know unless you try.

Passing Routes

Before you initiate action toward your destination, you need to decide how you will get there. Passing plays utilize a variety of routes the receiver might run to get into position to catch the ball. When you chart these passing routes, your diagram looks a little like a tree whose limbs are growing out of control. The trunk is firm and straight, but the branches veer off in all directions.

Let's have some fun with this.

Try giving a descriptive name to each of the plays numbered in the diagram. If you can, choose a short word, ideally a single word—after all, time is short for initiating a play on the field! Ready, set (set down the book and take as much time as you need) ... and go.

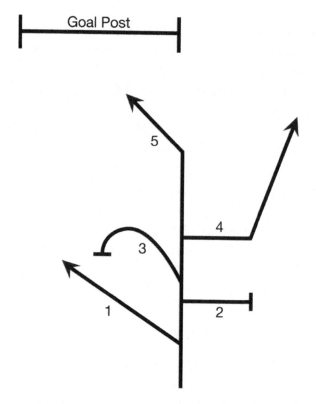

If you couldn't come up with a name for each of the routes, no worries. Let's try another approach. Below is a list of the play names in the diagram. Match the number of the route to the play name.

___Post
___Hook
___Out
___Corner
___Slant

How'd you do? These routes, represented by the limb-like directional arrows, are some of the ways a receiver might rendezvous with the ball. There could be a variety of ways for you to reach your goal. Taking the time to identify options is always a smart play.

Play-Action Pass

You wouldn't think that football, with its heavyweight players, is a sleight-of-hand kind of sport. But it tries to be. Remember the draw running play? The offense fakes a pass then ends up running the ball. That same "sleight of hand" happens with a few passing plays. Probably the most popular is the play-action pass. In the play-action pass, the quarterback fakes a hand-off to a runner and then passes the ball to a receiver.

What's interesting about the play-action pass, sometimes called the play-pass, is the teamwork involved. In the first few seconds of the play, the quarterback fakes a hand-off to a running back and the offensive line blocks as though opening a gap for the runner to pass through. Each player is focused on setting up for a run. After a few steps, and once the defensive line gets wise, the receivers break off and run their route to receive the ball, while the offensive line switches to defending the quarterback from the rushing defense.

Next time you watch a game, listen for the announcer to identify a "play-action pass," and then watch the replay to track the players.

A Wing and a Prayer

Sometimes football passing plays have to be loose and creative to do a job such as throwing off the defense to get a first down, or making a last-ditch effort to score in the final seconds of a game. Introducing the flea flicker pass and the Hail Mary. Believe me, you don't have to hate fleas to like the flea flicker play and you don't have to be religious to appreciate the Hail Mary.

The flea flicker play looks pretty wicked on a chart but can be fun to watch in a game. The ball is hiked to the quarterback who tosses it, like a hot potato, to a running back just behind him. The running back runs forward a few steps and then throws the ball back to the quarterback who has now dropped back behind the running back. At that point, the QB throws the ball downfield to a receiver or sneaks in a short run. It's just enough of a surprise to pick up a first down. The play was created in 1910 by Bob Zuppke and named after the quick flicking motion of a dog getting rid of fleas. You can watch a YouTube video of flea flicker plays on my website Extras page (www.LipstickFootball.com/extras).

A Hail Mary is a last-resort play usually saved for the final seconds of a game when the offense is one score away from winning but is nowhere close to the end zone. It isn't always effective but, when it is, often goes down in the record books. Unlike the flea flicker, a Hail Mary is pretty simple. The ball is hiked and the quarterback lingers in the pocket as long as possible, buying time for any and all receivers to run to the end zone, then lets loose the longest pass he can throw. By the time the ball reaches the end zone, a large group of offensive *and* defensive players have gathered to try to catch the ball. If an offensive player can pluck it out of the air, their team scores for the win.

In 2015, in the final few seconds of the game between the Green Bay Packers and the Detroit Lions, Packers quarterback Aaron Rodgers threw an amazing 61-yard pass which won the game for the Packers. The play itself was dubbed "The Miracle in Motown." It was a miracle Rodgers threw it that far and that a receiver caught it. And it all happened in the city still called by the nickname derived from the descriptors "Motor Town" or "Motor City" that applied to Detroit in the days when it was the global center of the automotive industry.

Defensive Strategies

Theft and prevention. These two words are often used together in the context of a robbery. How do you steal something? The flip side of that is—how do you protect something valuable from being stolen? Together, theft and prevention sum up the defensive strategy in a football game. If the valuable is the football itself, then the defense has two jobs: if not stealing the football from the opponent's offense, then at least preventing the offense from moving it downfield. Success with either of these options will give their team the ball and another opportunity to score.

How does the defense go about their theft and prevention? As football thieves, they place themselves in front of receivers to catch or intercept an incoming pass. They relentlessly work at forcing running backs to fumble the ball, creating a change of possession and getting their offense back on the field. To prevent their opponent's offense from making forward progress, the defense rushes across the line to sack the quarterback before completing a pass to a receiver.

The defense does not come to a match empty-handed. They come with a specific strategy based on what they've observed their opponent do in previous games and what they anticipate they'll try in the current game. And like the offense, they might change or adapt their strategy according to how the game is evolving.

A well-rehearsed general strategy can also be effective. Tim DeRuyter, Defensive Coordinator of the Oregon Ducks, drills his players on the four Ps, which he feels helps them play in a "flow" state. (More on flow and mental conditioning in chapter 9.) The four Ps are:

Population	Get more of their players to the ball
Physicality	Punch, rip, strip and go after the football
Purpose	Don't just make a tackle, take the ball away
Preparation	Know your defense well enough to disguise things

Like quarterbacks who have the benefit of a communication device in their helmets, one defensive player can wear a device to receive input and direction from the team's defensive coach or coordinator throughout the game.

To put the defense in their place, let's take a closer look at their formations and types of coverage.

Defensive Formations

As you learned in chapter 5, the defense focuses on covering two areas of the field—where the play begins and where it might end in the backfield. The defensive front includes seven linemen and linebackers who cover the action around the line of scrimmage. The secondary includes two corners and two safeties who cover the backfield to intercept passes or shut down break-out runs.

The defensive front can line up in a variety of ways. One of the most common ways is the 4-3 formation with four linemen on the line of scrimmage and three linebackers behind them. That formation puts a lot of power at the LOS. That lineup can be switched to the 3-4 position, placing three linemen on the line of scrimmage and four linebackers behind them, creating a strong back-up system should an offensive running back get past the linemen.

When the offense just needs one yard to convert to another set of downs, you might see the defensive front move into a 5-2 formation, which puts the muscle of five linemen at the line of scrimmage, leaving two linebackers to fill in the gaps. This formation can also be used for a *blitz*, where defensive players rush in to tackle the quarterback or interrupt a pass attempt. In a blitz, there are more defensive players on the line than offensive players.

If the play looks to be a long pass, the defense might move into the *nickel defense* formation. In this lineup, one of the linebackers drops back, adding a fifth person to beef up the secondary in the backfield.

Although *your* job in life is to initiate offensive action on your plays, understanding potential defensive moves is an important part of the process. When you start to recognize a defensive strategy, whether coming from other people or yourself, you can adapt your play accordingly or initiate a different play altogether. Remember, a defensive play in life is meant to either steal your ball or stop you from making forward progress towards your goal. Don't be caught off guard.

Defensive Coverage

When you watch a televised football game, you don't always get to see how the defense is lining up in the backfield. Instead, the camera focuses on the front line to follow the quarterback's actions. When the camera cuts to a wide shot, or when you watch a game from the stands, you see where the defensive players line up before the play begins. That tells you which of the two primary approaches the defense is using to cover receivers—man-to-man or zone coverage.

You can probably guess the difference between the two. In man-to-man, you play Tammy Wynette singing "Stand By Your Man" in your head. Wherever "your man" goes, you go. If he runs downfield, you run after him. Whatever "your man" does, you do. If he leaps into the air to catch a pass, you either leap and try to catch the ball yourself or make sure "your man" doesn't catch it. When the offense decides to send all five eligible receivers downfield, a nickel defense playing man-to-man ensures each receiver will be covered.

The other approach to defense is zone coverage, which is about covering a territory of the field rather than an individual player. Its primary purpose is to protect against the pass—short and long. When the ball is hiked and put into motion, the defensive backers (corners and safeties) drop back and defend against any receivers in their territory or zone who might catch a deep pass. Likewise, linebackers or defensive ends closer to the line of scrimmage might be assigned a zone to protect against a short pass. Zone coverage is a way for a team to expand coverage across the field.

What do the defensive forces in your own life look like? When you take action, do you feel blocked by an individual? If so, you're staring down a man-to-man defensive formation. If you feel blocked by situations or circumstances, you're looking at a zone defense. By becoming aware of the types of defensive forces blocking you, you can adjust your plays or choose alternative actions that will help you overcome—or at least slip around—who or what is in your way.

Huddle Up

Wilma Rudolph was an American sprinter, Olympian champion and sports icon. In 1960, she became the first American woman to win three gold medals in a single Olympic Games—for the 100- and 200-meter individual events and the 4 x 100-meter relay. She was pronounced "the fastest woman in the world." Yet in 1945, at the age of five, she had been living a different reality. She had contracted polio and was strapped into a leg brace that she needed until she was 12. At an early age, Wilma was faced with two possibilities—would she walk again or not? "My doctor told me I would never walk again," said Wilma. "My mother told me I would. I believed my mother."

Football is a highly competitive game. Is competition always a good thing? Seattle Seahawks coach Pete Carroll thinks it is. In his book *Win Forever: Live, Work, and Play Like a Champion*, he says, "If you want to win forever, always compete." The thing is, if you're out on the field pushing a dream on your own, who do you compete with? Coach Carroll answers that one as well. "The only competition that matters is the one that takes place within yourself. It isn't about external factors." Wilma Rudolph knew that all too well. She started becoming a fierce competitor the moment she decided she didn't want to just walk but run, race and win.

Sometimes you take action and feel foolish because your play didn't work. Who cares? The next one will. To be your best self, compete with yourself. Challenge yourself. When you get into the habit of initiating action time and again, you *will* accomplish your goal.

Break It Down

Initiating action is something that gets easier the more you do it. However tough that first attempt might be, give it a second or third try. In the next chapter, you will learn more about the power of repetition. For now, practice initiating action toward your goal.

FOOTBALL

1. As you watch a game, track the offensive plays. Start by saying out loud to yourself "run," "pass," or "fake."

2. Listen for what the quarterback says to initiate the play and hike the ball. What do you hear? Numbers? Colors? Hike? Hut? Someone's name?

3. Watch a defensive cornerback follow a receiver downfield. Remember, theft (of ball) and prevention (of forward progress) is what the defense is all about.

4. As you're watching a game, draw some of the receivers' passing routes. Do you recognize any of them? Can you name them?

5. When you hear an announcer talk about zone vs. man-to-man coverage, key into the play or replay so you can see how the defensive players line up.

LIFE

1. Consider one of your long-range (distal) goals. Make a list of short-term proximal goals that will help you get there. What actions can you take to reach one of those proximal goals?

2. A quarterback says "Hut" to initiate a play. Create a personal audible to spur you into action. It could be your favorite color or birthday numbers. Maybe "Green–13–Hut." Or "Red–21–Hike." Or simply, "Go, baby, go!"

3. When you're ready, set a 40-second play clock. And then press Start. Before it expires, say your audible then initiate action—on something.

4. Create a music play list that will make initiating action fun. Mine is old-school, but it works for me. It includes Queen's "We Are the Champions," "Katy Perry's "Roar," and the theme from *Rocky*.

5. If you don't already know the 1983 hit song "Jump" by the Pointer Sisters, listen to it—then do it. The act of jumping reduces feelings of anxiety and thaws your "frozen" periods, allowing you to re-engage with your work and initiate more plays in your life.

Chapter 8

CONDITION

Building Routines

We are what we repeatedly do.
Excellence, then, is not an act, but a habit.

—Aristotle, Greek Philosopher

When you read the word "mastery," what do you think of? Merriam-Webster says mastery is the "possession or display of great skill or technique, skill or knowledge that makes one master of a subject." And the masters themselves? Fame places some on a pedestal. As you look up at them, it may seem the best-known masters were *born* with their "great skill or technique."

Angela Duckworth, in her book *Grit: The Power of Passion and Perseverance,* poses a question that challenges that societal norm: "Why do we assume it is our talent rather than our effort that will decide where we end up in the very long run?" By examining her students' efforts in the classroom, Duckworth found something quite useful. "The focus on talent distracts us from something that is at least as important, and that's effort. As any coach or athlete will tell you, consistency of effort over the long run is everything. As much as talent counts, effort counts twice."

Developing any talent—through effort and perseverance—is how you become a master or become good at what you want to do. Martial arts master Bruce Lee was keenly aware of the power of perseverance. "I fear not the man who has practiced 10,000 kicks once," Lee said, "but I fear the man who has practiced one kick 10,000 times." You see a similar fierceness on a football field. Players work tirelessly to drill and hone actions until they can perform them without thinking.

Although developing your talent starts by committing yourself, there can be no outcome from commitment without follow-up. I like to think of this as "rehearsing your life." You're here, so you've committed to life. But it's the actions you're taking—in this very moment—that determine how your life will evolve. Maybe not this minute, but next month or next year.

As you intentionally condition yourself, by choosing what you repeatedly do both mentally and physically and how you do it, you exercise significant influence as the director of your life's performance.

Introducing the C Principle – Condition

Condition is both a noun and a verb. As a noun, it refers to the state of something, for example, what condition your lawn mower is in. I'm going to use it, like all other LIPSTICK Football principles, as a verb, as something you do. You condition your body by repeating physical actions. You condition your mind by repeating thoughts.

You've heard the old joke . . . "Tourist: How do I get to Carnegie Hall? New Yorker: "*Practice, practice, practice!*" But don't laugh.

When I was working on my music degree, I was a piano major and had to reach a certain level of proficiency to graduate. I loved piano, had a natural talent for it and shined when I played.

During my first three years in college, however, I focused my time and attention on accompanying a University pop group. Unlike my classical music-loving peers, my roots were in pop music, so I felt comfortable in that role. That is, until my new piano teacher gave me a "C" at the end of the semester. I was shocked. I thought my rehearsal schedule of one hour a day, five days a week was pretty darned good. My teacher didn't agree. "You can't get better if you don't commit yourself," he said.

"Okay," I asked, "What would it take to get better?" Of course, what I was really wondering was what it would take to get a better grade. My teacher said, "Practice three hours every day." The only time I could schedule three hours in a grand piano practice room was from 7-10 a.m. And so, after practicing at the crack of dawn every day of the semester, my grade went from a C... to a B? What? Again, I was perplexed—and whined to my teacher. "I showed up and practiced three hours every day. And I only made a B?" To which my teacher channeled a Zen master with "You made good progress." I felt a "but" coming. "But you didn't apply yourself during the practice sessions as much as you could." What I hadn't realized was that it would take more than committing time toward a goal. I had to commit attention, too.

I was disappointed and felt like throwing in the towel. Instead, I hung in there and asked my teacher for guidance. As the Zen wisdom goes, when the student is ready, the teacher will appear. And I was ready. Committing to that *amount* of practice time prepared me for the next step, which was where the big payoff was—taking control of my piano skills. I followed my teacher's instructions to divide and conquer by breaking down each piano piece into segments. He taught me the physics of how to strike a key, move fingers independently, and change dynamics in subtle ways—and master one musical phrase at a time.

By the end of that semester, I was an A student, although getting an A grade was no longer my priority. What mattered more was that I'd learned how to prepare and perform a handful of piano pieces masterfully. Not because of any huge amount of talent I brought into the rehearsal room, and not because I committed to being in the room three hours a day, which was a prerequisite. It was because of the perseverance and determination I applied while I was *in* that room. As I worked hard to change the tiniest of habits, I conditioned myself to play better. Angela Duckworth was right. "As much as talent counts, effort counts twice."

The remarkable thing is that your efforts don't have to be huge as you chip away at your goal. They can be small, but they have to be consistent. Sociologist Dan Chambliss observed in one of his studies, "Superlative performance is really a confluence of dozens of small skills or activities, each one learned or stumbled upon, which have been carefully drilled into habit and then fitted together in a synthesized whole. There's nothing extraordinary or superhuman in any one of those actions. Only the fact that they are done consistently and correctly. And altogether produce excellence." One kick—performed correctly—10,000 times.

Becoming a master doesn't have to be your ultimate goal. You can simply want to live your best life. To do that, you must take responsibility for your own conditioning and develop intentional habits that align with your dreams, goals and values. Decide which actions you want to keep repeating, change those you don't, and build routines that fulfill your potential—in all areas of life. Don't worry if you don't know how to divide and conquer just yet. I'll channel my brilliant—and patient—piano teacher to help "break it down."

The Condition principle can be applied on and off the field. So, rather than cover another aspect of playing football, I'm going to focus on how conditioning is used throughout football, starting with how the NFL league evolved. I'll also teach you, in steps, how to catch a football. If you take that instruction it should prove that, with consistent effort, you can condition yourself to do anything you put your mind to. Along the way, you'll meet an NFL coach who utilized the "C" Principle to get his team to the Super Bowl, not once but twice.

American (Gridiron) Football

Mention football anywhere in the world outside of North America and you'll be starting a conversation about soccer. Google the word "football," and you get links to soccer websites. That's because soccer, which is called football outside of America, is the world's biggest sport. Its fan base exceeds 3.5 *billion*. In a Top Ten list of the world's most popular sports, with soccer at #1, football ties basketball for #9 with a measly 400 million fans. From this position, it might look as though football either fell from favor or was never blessed to begin with. Neither is true.

American football, also referred to as gridiron football, evolved from two sports—soccer and rugby. The first match was in 1869 between two American colleges, Rutgers and Princeton. If you had watched that game, you'd think you were watching a soccer match—with the ball always in motion. Rules are, after all, a form of conditioning and players learned to play by that game's set of rules.

In 1880, a man named Walter Camp—player, coach and sportswriter—came up with a different approach to the game. He tweaked the rules so players could take a brief break between actions. To do that, he created the down system to separate plays, the hike or snap to start a play, the line of scrimmage, and the necessity of having eleven members in each play—all aspects of the game as it's played today.

When Walt defined this new approach, new rules were created, and American football was born. It may have taken a while for players to get the hang of the new game, but—over time and through repetition—they did. Walter's influence on the game was so profound, he's often called "the father of American football."

NFL—Divide and Conquer

In 1920, about 40 years after Walter Camp put his unique stamp on the game, the American Professional Football

Association, the APFA, was formed with 14 teams. The first president was Olympian extraordinaire Jim Thorpe. Two years later, in 1922, the APFA had grown to include 18 teams and was renamed the National Football League.

In the early 1940s, during WWII, the NFL grew and expanded. To create organizational structure within the league, it created two divisions—Eastern and Western divisions. But like all good sports, the NFL had rival football leagues, one of which was the American Football League, or AFL. The AFL became a serious challenger during the 1960s. By 1969, the AFL had 10 teams while the NFL had 16. In 1970, the two leagues, with a total of 26 teams, merged into one league and the NFL as we know it today was born. And if you're counting years, the NFL celebrates its 100th anniversary in 2022.

As part of the new league structure, two conferences were created—the American Football Conference and the National Football Conference—the AFC and the NFC. Half the NFL teams are in each conference, and each has its own logo. The AFC logo is red and the NFC logo is blue.

Both logos have four white stars that represent the four geographical divisions in each conference—North, South, East and West. The NFL logo, which is red and blue, has eight stars— four on either side of the football. These represent the eight divisions in the National Football League.

Let's divide and conquer the divisions and conferences. Today, there are 32 teams in the NFL:

1 – League (NFL)
2 – Conferences (AFC and NFC)
8 – Divisions (four in each conference)
4 – Teams in each division

Enough math for now. In chapter 9, you'll learn how a team earns its way into a playoff position and ultimately into the Super Bowl.

Conditioned to Watch

Here today, gone tomorrow. Football fans await the season impatiently, only to feel it's over almost before it's begun. In contrast, the National Basketball Association (NBA) seems to go on forever. Starting in the fall, NBA teams play 82 games during the regular season, and playoffs continue into the summer. Major League Baseball? MLB teams generally play 162 games a season.

The NFL season, the shortest of all sports, is a rather sweet yet fleeting 17-week season. Each team plays one game per week—either a home game or a road game. They used to play just 16 games with a week off somewhere during the season. As of 2021, teams will play a full 17-game season. No coveted week off or "bye."

Soccer may have more fans, but NFL football on television brings that sport more broadcasting and advertising income than any other. The first televised NFL game was covered by NBC network on October 22nd, 1939. After WWII, home entertainment gradually became synonymous with television, and televised football became the number one form of home entertainment. By the early 1960s, it was a weekly televised event.

Most games are played on Sundays, allowing the largest viewing audience on both the east and west coasts, but weeknight football has a huge audience as well. Monday Night Football—or MNF—was introduced in 1970, the year of the NFL-AFL merger. The new kid on the TV block is Thursday Night Football, which started on Thanksgiving Day, 2006.

Remember, repeating an action over and over again will condition anyone to do almost anything. And that includes learning when to tune into your favorite sport.

General Conditioning

Football is a conditioning extravaganza. It's how teams are made, how games are won, and how players become superstars. But not all conditioning is the same. Of course, there's mental and physical conditioning. The first trains your mind to think in a certain way. And the second trains your body to act in a certain way.

There are also two levels of conditioning—general and specific. Aerobic exercise, such as jogging, biking or swimming, is a general way to achieve physical stamina and flexibility. Lifting weights strengthens a specific muscle or muscle group.

Psychological and mental conditioning can also be general or specific. Thinking or saying a positive affirmation or uplifting thought such as "I can do it" makes you feel better in general. Saying (even gasping) "I can run one more mile" can motivate you to reach a specific target.

Let's focus on general conditioning. From the very first practice, football teams work hard to improve overall physical and mental conditioning. Some drills increase strength and flexibility or develop faster sprinting times. Others build mental focus and determination. "Who are we?" the coach asks the team in a locker room break. "We're invincible," comes a unified response from the team. Or, "We're unstoppable." Or a back-and-forth chant:

"Whose house?"

"Our house."

"Whose house?"

"*OUR* house."

You get the idea. (You can watch an entertaining YouTube video compilation of pregame chants on my website Extras page.) When players repeat or chant a phrase over and over, it builds belief in their team's overall ability. The chants don't prep a player for a skilled physical move but rather create a mental zone of positive expectation which is a good place to begin a game—or any task, for that matter. If positive affirmations are a practice you have embraced in life as players do in a sport, you benefit from general conditioning the way they do by repeating supportive, positive statements of well-being.

General conditioning is how a coach motivates and directs the team to an aspiration, a way to think about themselves. Some coaches develop a personal coaching philosophy they carry with them over the years. Coach Pete Carroll's core philosophy is simple and very much aligned with the C Principle: "Practice is everything."

General conditioning won't prepare you to catch the ball better or master a piano piece. But if a team chant, or someone's praise ringing in your ear or mind, or even a wise one-liner puts you in a positive mental zone—whether on a football field or in a rehearsal room—and if it makes you want to commit to mastering something, then, mission accomplished!

Micro Conditioning

While general conditioning prepares the soil, the next step—choosing which seeds to plant—has to be specific, otherwise the fruits of your labor won't produce what you expect. Is there a level of conditioning beyond specific? Yes! It's your lucky day, because this is where I channel my college piano teacher and introduce you to *micro* conditioning—a level beyond specific.

Micro conditioning is how you perfect a play—on the field and off. It's the level I had to reach to master my piano pieces and it's exactly how you can grow the seeds in your own fertile soil. Mastering any new skill requires micro conditioning, which is where "divide and conquer" comes in. To perfect an action, you break it down into "micro" steps (divide), then practice, drill, polish, hone or rehearse those steps until you've mastered each one (conquer). When I coach, I like to say, "When you hone it, you own it."

Diamond or cross. Tuck and run. In a following section of this chapter, I will keep my promise to tell you how to catch a football. Diamond for a high catch. Cross for a low grab. Then tuck and run. But how do you make that high catch? While you can target improvement of a specific action such as catching a football, micro conditioning hones the exact skills needed to catch that ball—what finger or hand goes where and does what.

Let's recap:

General Conditioning > Play better football

Specific Conditioning > Catch the ball

Micro Conditioning > Perfect the high catch

The tricky thing about conditioning is that it happens whether you choose it or not. Aristotle was right—we are what we repeatedly do. If you aren't paying attention in your own rehearsal or practice session, whatever that may look like, you could end up repeating old habits or patterns that don't serve you well. You have to step away from the expectation that your talent will, or should, see you through. Remember, talent is just the beginning. Your real journey begins when you start claiming the full extent of your talent. To do that, you have to keep a close eye on *how* you're practicing or rehearsing your life, and always remain a vigilant student.

When you rehearse and repeat micro actions, they lead to habitual *reactions*, or habits. To take a closer look at habits and the micro-conditioning process, I want to introduce a former NFL coach and Pro Football Hall of Fame honoree who demonstrated the effectiveness of micro conditioning.

Coach Dungy on Micro Conditioning

"My language was terrible when I was younger," explains Coach Dungy, retired ex-coach of the Indianapolis Colts. "But once I realized, if I wasn't careful, that would really become who I am, I made a decision to stop."

Early in life, Tony Dungy learned he could change his unwanted habits and behaviors. Over the years, he developed that ability and integrated it into his coaching. When Dungy came to the Indiana Colts as head coach in 2002, he inherited a strong offense with Peyton Manning in the quarterback position. The defense, however, wasn't as strong.

Dungy wanted his defense to act faster. He knew if they could increase their speed by just a few milliseconds, his defense would get the upper hand on a play. A defensive linebacker could penetrate the line and rush the quarterback. That would force the quarterback to get rid of the ball faster and make the receivers downfield scramble into position sooner. And that would give

Dungy's defensive backs and safeties more time to possibly intercept the pass. In general, it would throw off the offense—a strategy Coach Dungy believed could win games.

Rather than change everything about what the big "D" was doing, Dungy dropped the thick playbooks and focused on converting just a few plays into habits. Since defensive players often wait and react to what the offense does, Dungy drilled the habit of stepping into position immediately—as soon as the ball was hiked. He wanted to remove the hesitancy of waiting and then reacting to what the offense was doing. He wanted his players to act instinctively.

Of course, belief plays a big role in any major change. Think about it. When you're under pressure and there's a hesitancy about how to do something new, you will always fall back on familiar behavior. Through Dungy's tireless efforts, he earned the trust of his players as he relieved them of the burden of thought. They no longer had to choose what to do and where to move when the play began. Dungy made that decision for them. The players just had to rehearse and drill their action until it was automatic—until it became a habit.

As Dungy explains, "Champions don't do extraordinary things. They do ordinary things, but they do them without thinking—too fast for the other team to react. They follow the habits they've learned."

Catch the Damn Ball

Let's break for a micro football drill. Repeat after me: *Diamonds* are a girl's best friend. *Cross* my heart.

I've just given you two touchstone words and phrases you can use to rehearse how to catch a football—the right way. Diamond and cross. While we're at it, here are two more: tuck and run. I'll tell you more about those in a minute.

With two pointy ends, a football isn't always easy to catch. If it's thrown hard, it can slip through your fingers, hit your chest or arms, and leave you zingers and bruises you'll be nursing for days. Believe me, I know. And if it drops, it doesn't just bounce back up into your hands, the way a round basketball does. A football's oblong shape causes it to bounce in unexpected ways, usually away from you and often into the hands of your opponent. Not good. So, how do you catch a football?

When the football is coming at you above your head, where you might wear a diamond tiara, you use the *diamond* catch. Extend your arms, hands facing out above shoulder height— fingers pointing up. Touch thumbs together, then pointer fingers together, to create a diamond shape. Creating that diamond shape keeps the ball from slipping through your hands.

To catch a low ball, extend your arms, hands *below* shoulder height facing up —fingers pointing down. Cross your pinkie finger tips to create a web with your hands. Of course, choosing the diamond or cross has to be a quick decision. But the more you practice both options, the sooner you'll instinctively pick one over the other.

Tuck and run. Once you catch the ball, you have to protect it. Tuck it quickly into either the left or right side of your chest, with the tip of the football secured in the palm of your hand and the ball pressed tightly against your forearm.

As you watch a game, see if you can recognize these moves. Then grab your own ball and do a little micro conditioning.

Under the Hood of a Habit

Psychologists estimate we spend between 40 and 95 percent of our daily lives performing habits. Without habits, our brains would be mush, overtaxed by constantly learning or relearning how to do something. That's why Coach Dungy chose drilling habits over studying a thick playbook.

Habits are essential to mental health. Remember when you were learning to drive a car? You had to think through individual steps. First brake, change gears, signal before turning, look both ways. Can you imagine burdening your brain with those individual steps each time you went for a drive today?

Some people talk about *breaking* a bad habit. If you look under the hood of a habit, as many psychologists have in recent years, you'll find what they found—a habit is not so much breakable as it is changeable. In Charles Duhigg's bestselling book *The Power of Habit: Why We Do What We Do in Life and Business,* he introduces the concept that a single habit has three parts or components, yet only one is under your control. While I agree with Duhigg's theory and highly recommend his book for a deeper dive, I'm going to diverge by simply renaming those three parts.

I've just given an example of how driving a car can become an automatic process after many years of practice. Here's something further about a car—*my* car, spelled C.A.R. I spell car this way to reinforce the three parts of a habit. Let's take a closer look under the hood of a C.A.R.

C is for Cue.

Think about one of your habits. Let's say it's eating an afternoon "pick-me-up" snack. What makes you want that snack? If you're at your work desk, do you start to doze off? Do you feel sluggish? Does your mind drift? Is it harder to focus? These are various cues. When something along those lines happens, your next thought might be, "I need a break." So, after being triggered by the Cue, you take Action.

A is for Action.

There are thousands of actions you could take in response to a particular cue. For example, once you recognize you're in an afternoon slump, do you give in to the urge to eat something fun—a cookie, a donut or some chips? Something to "treat" yourself for working so hard? Or maybe you turn to something nutritious like a piece of fruit. Whatever you do in response to the Cue is your habitual Action—what you think of as your habit.

R is for Reward.

After taking action, what Reward did you get? Your first thought might be that you satisfied your sweet tooth with a cookie. Or got nutrients from a piece of fruit. Maybe you added steps to your step counter or called a friend to make a plan for the evening. No matter the action, the real Reward is—you got a break from work.

What if your habit stops being productive? Perhaps your afternoon Cue leads to eating something sweet every day. After a while, you start gaining weight, which might not be desirable. What do you do? Rather than try to break the habit cycle, you replace your Action, your *response* to the Cue, with something healthier or more productive—meditate, read, do yoga stretches or take a brisk walk around the block.

If you're not happy with your habits, look at them from the C.A.R. perspective. And consider changing a tire here or there to make sure they get you where you want to go.

The Action Evolution

Since I've dragged you under the hood of a habit, let's look at how to divide and conquer that Action component. Does it always start with a physical action? Coach Dungy wanted to change his bad language. Did his bad language originate with words? Or did his words evolve from how he felt and thought about himself as a young man? Conditioning happens over time, so it's not always easy to know exactly what needs fixing. You have to examine the "action evolution"—how a feeling morphs into a thought, then words, then physical action.

The action evolution can happen fast. Let a negative thought slide by enough times and you'll eventually express that thought verbally, and then one day act on it. Even stating what you want and following it with a contrary "...but I can't because..." creates confusion and starts an emotional tug of war. To replace an unwanted Action in one of your habits, you first have to find where it originates along the action evolution line. Is it a feeling?

A thought you keep repeating in your mind? Competing thoughts? Once you find and replace it with a more productive Action—it's smooth sailing.

"Repeat after me," I said to myself: "I am confident and secure at the helm of a 22-foot Catalina sailboat." More than anything, I wanted to pass muster and be accepted into the Fairwind Yacht Club, a small no-frills, co-op-style sailing club in Southern California. Not having years of sailing experience as many in the club did, my confidence was listing. I had sailing skill; I just didn't *feel* as if I did. To change that feeling, I crafted the specific statement above to state unequivocally how I wanted to think mentally and feel emotionally at the helm. By repeating that statement over and over, with great vim and vigor, I conditioned myself to believe it. Within a few weeks, as I changed my habit of thinking, my confidence grew to match my skills.

It's not that our brains are stupid. They just have to be taught how to be smart. And if the only input we give our brains is to confirm bad behavior or low expectations, then we are giving way too much control to that small but mighty three-pound mass of gray matter that contains 85 billion neurons firing left, right and center.

Those neurons, if not clearly directed, can lead to a pretty heavy traffic jam or bottleneck—sometimes near misses and other times outright collisions of thought and intent. Coach Dungy's defensive line didn't believe their quick actions would make that much difference—until Dungy's clearly focused plan of attack started winning games. One kick, 10,000 times.

When you look at the evolution of your actions, you supercharge your micro-conditioning process. And that gray matter in your head? You get to be the boss of it—not the other way around. As F. Matthias Alexander, creator of the Alexander Technique, said, "People do not decide their futures, they decide their habits and their habits decide their futures."

A Matter of Routine

If a well-maintained C.A.R. can help you reach your goal, what could a fleet of cars do for you?

"Hut 1. Hut 2. Hike!" Once the offense hears the magic Cue word, they initiate a play. The center hikes the ball, guards and tackles block while quarterback drops back, running back rushes by, quarterback fakes a handoff, finds an open receiver downfield and throws the ball. Reward? Yardage and (the team hopes) a new set of downs.

A football play isn't just one action. It's a series of individual actions combined into a routine. A routine could be anything, really—a string of dance steps, a specific order of jokes, a performer's set list, your morning activities, even dog tricks. My dog has a routine—sit, stay, down, roll over, high five, shake, fetch. She can do a dozen different tricks in a row. OK, so she's not that great at fetch. The point is, once she learns a few tricks in a specific order, she repeats them in that order. I'm not making a judgment on her intelligence. She's brilliant, I'm sure.

We humans are similar in that we become familiar with doing things in a particular order. First this, then that, then the other. And voilà—a routine is formed. You create routines all the time. Sometimes it's knowingly and intentionally, the way a professional comic, performer or football team might. More often than not, routines are formed more passively, simply by repeating a series of actions—one after the other—for a repeated length of time…say…all your life.

Habits, and habitual actions like driving a car, can relieve your brain from relearning tasks. Well-formed routines can take an even bigger load off your mind by reducing decision fatigue. The act of making a decision—even if those decisions are simple or inconsequential—can deplete your willpower and wear down your ability to make other decisions. Implementing routines, however, can delay decision fatigue and reserve valuable brain energy for important tasks you'll face later in the day.

Before taking office, then President-elect Barack Obama created routines he knew would save brain power. "You need to focus your decision-making energy. You need to routinize yourself," said Obama. In a 2012 Vanity Fair profile, Michael Lewis described the morning routines Obama intentionally created to save decision-making effort. "You'll see I wear only gray or blue suits," Obama said. "I'm trying to pare down decisions. I don't want to make decisions about what I'm eating or wearing. Because I have too many other decisions to make."

An NFL team is a "routine machine." Each day of the week has a focus that leads up to the big game. Seattle Seahawks Coach Pete Carrol has a different theme for each day, such as Tell the Truth Mondays (review the weekend game) and Turnover Wednesdays (practice protecting the ball).

In the article "NFL Players in Their Own Words," players describe their personal routines for each day of the week. Fred Beasley, former San Francisco 49ers running back, says: "I try to do things at the exact same time every week, so I won't have a lot of time to sit there and do nothing. This game is 70 percent mental and 30 percent physical."

You don't have to be POTUS or an NFL player to experience decision fatigue. If you experience it, re-condition your routines. Remember, a routine is just a sequence of habits: actions you've conditioned yourself to perform. No matter what habits you string together or in what order—get up, work out, write, go to work, rehearse, walk the dog, make coffee, eat breakfast, meditate—if you design the routine with intention, you'll find yourself in the company of some pretty high-level operators and Super Bowl winning teams.

Huddle Up

Life is full of choices. Although you don't get to choose the amount of talent you are born with, you can choose to pick up the ball that's handed to you and run with it. And, like a water drip that changes the face of a stone over time, how you carry that ball toward your goal will be a direct reflection of how you condition yourself—what you choose to repeatedly feel, think, say and do. It's your choice.

Don't let the idea that you are short of talent keep you from developing the skills you *do* have. And whatever it is you're reaching for, dreaming about, or imagining you can do or become, remember Angela Duckworth's challenge: "As much as talent counts, effort counts twice. Consistency of effort over the long run is everything." So there! You have just as much right to catch the damned ball as anyone else does.

Break It Down

If you're not sure where to step in, try the divide-and-conquer approach in these steps to hone your actions and bring them into alignment with your goals.

FOOTBALL

1. What's a good day in your typical week for watching football? Start a routine of watching on that day. Or maybe even throwing the ball with a friend.

2. As you're watching a game, reinforce your knowledge about the two NFL conferences. Are you hearing or seeing the name of the conference each team is in?

3. Divide and conquer your football knowledge. Pick one aspect or position and add it to your game-watching routine. Once you're comfortable with it, change focus to a different aspect of the game.

4. Earlier in the chapter, I taught you how to catch a football. How do you throw one? And how do you throw a "spiral"? A lot of physical mechanics goes into throwing the ball properly—grip, stance, finger position, release. A video on my Extras page shows one way to do it (www.LipstickFootball.com/extras).

LIFE

1. Pick one personal habit and break it down into its components—Cue, Action, and Reward. Be patient. It takes persistence to recognize the mechanics of a habit.

2. If you're happy with that habit, acknowledge it. If you don't feel it's serving you well, think about other Actions that would support you better. Then try a few and see which you like best.

3. Identify a morning or evening routine and list the habits within that routine. Are you happy with each of them? If not, identify those that may be slowing you down or keeping your routine from being effective. Then repeat step 2.

4. Words can be powerful. If you have a habit of adding the contrary conjunction "but" to some of your goal-oriented statements, you'll enjoy the "I Love You... But" exercise from my upcoming book, *LIPSTICK FOOTBALL Workbook*. If you want to kick those "buts" to the sidelines, download the free exercise here: www.LipstickFootball.com/action.

Chapter 9

KICK

Women in Football

All you can do is just continue to grind, continue to work, and show everybody what you're capable of.

—Katie Sowers, Former NFL Assistant Coach
for the San Francisco 49ers

Walk with me. You're in a long, bright hallway with lots of closed doors. This is your present. One of the doors leads you to your destination, your future. Call it your dream or vision room if you like. It's where you go to imagine and visualize what you want next—a goal, a dream job, a new skill. You instinctively stop at what you realize is *your* room. Excitedly, you reach for the door handle and open the door.

What you see is so beautiful it takes your breath away. It's everything you've wanted and hoped for. You look around and see images and articles that proclaim you've accomplished your goal. Remember, this room is your future. You step in to immerse yourself in this new reality. You pull the door behind you, but it doesn't close. You don't know why until you look down and see there's a foot on the doorsill.

You are looking at that unhelpful appendage, your foot of fear. If this intrusion into your vision room is not fear of failure or a shortage of belief in yourself, it could be a weight you've been carrying: a disappointment, limits that have started closing in on you, a missed opportunity for which you blame yourself. Whatever it is to you, like a defensive linebacker trying to force you to fumble, it's determined to block your forward progress and make you give up on your dreams. In reality, that intrusive foot is simply a past-tense residual that wants to distract you from your present-tense goals and future possibilities.

How do you remove the foot of fear? You shift your focus back to your dream room, to what you want, to what's in front of you—not what's behind you, what's blocking you or to what you don't want. That shift or kick forward has to be forceful, determined. Believe me, an offensive running back with the ball busting through the defensive line is not focused on the blockers directly in front but the bigger goal of the end zone downfield. What's your bigger goal? Focus on that.

In football, kicking a field goal can win a close game. In life, kicks are not so much external point makers as they are internal shift makers. When you shift position or perspective, you see things differently and free yourself to try something new. When you kick an obstacle to the curb, you clear a path for yourself to move forward. When you kick your own glass ceiling, you shatter your personal limitations. Whether it's a push, a nudge, or a kick in the butt, kicking is what pierces the veil of accomplishment. It's what carries you over the line—the finish line—of anything.

Introducing the K Principle – KICK

The moment I came into this world, I began exercising the Kick Principle. No one taught me how to kick—it's all my little legs could do once I took that first gulp of air after leaving the warm and watery safety of my mother's womb. To this day I feel a certain freedom when I'm in, on, or under any body of water. Being alive on the outside, however, is harder. There's gravity, for starters. Rules and regulations. Stop signs and dividers. People. It's not always easy to get where I want to go. When I think about how I arrived—kicking and probably screaming, I realize that's exactly what will get me through this physical life intact and on point.

To kick is an act of force. A kicker kicking a field goal takes a few steps back, gauges the wind, takes in the playing field and the players lined up on both sides of the ball, then runs up to the ball and kicks it. Even a punter gets into stride by taking a few skipping steps before drop kicking the ball downfield. Sometimes you ready yourself to act on something but then step back, let go or don't connect with the opportunity. You don't complete the kick. A forceful kick is one where you connect the runup to the kick itself.

To kick is an act of power. While a human punch has been clocked at about 44 mph, the velocity of a human kick has been recorded at 136 mph. Bruce Lee's kicks were so fast, a film camera couldn't capture the motion and, on the screen, it looked as if he hadn't kicked at all. In order for viewers to actually see his powerful moves, he had to slow down his kick. It was still so fast, the footage had to be slowed down as well.

The Kick Principle is 100% action, and not just in "do-or-die" moments in life, on the field or in a film. Kicking is much too valuable to reserve for those times alone. You should exercise the Kick Principle every day, but only if you use the power of your kick for good—for *your* good. Remember, it's not always the distance you move the ball. It's the *impact* of the effort. Even a small internal kick, which may take a huge kick-ass effort on your part, can be powerful enough to change your course of action— the same way a one-yard gain can turn around a football game.

What does it take for you to kick yourself into action? A gentle whisper? A nudge? A swift kick? If you're on the playing field, then you still want what's in the end zone, so keep kicking forward. Don't look back or kick yourself for not taking action. Kicking at what's past is wasted energy. Your power lies in this moment. You've already taken a leap to start your journey. Kicking is what you do every day to reach your destination. So, face forward, chin up, metaphorical shoulder pads on, give yourself a running start, then kick yourself into action. As Coach Katie Sowers says, "...continue to grind, continue to work, and show everybody what you're capable of."

In this chapter, I'll talk about champions and how they get to the Super Bowl. I'll talk about Wild Card teams and how they get into the playoffs. And I'll talk about women in football and how their kicks keep adding more cracks to the professional football glass ceiling. I'll also talk about the power of visualizing and how each kick, whether mental or physical, will help you build belief in yourself and your ability to take action on what you want.

The Kick principle needs exercising. So, suit up. You've got some kicking to do.

The Playoffs

How does an NFL team kick its way into the playoffs? To review, there are 32 NFL teams divided into two national conferences—the American Football Conference (AFC) and the National Football Conference (NFC). Each conference represents four geographical divisions—North, South, East and West, with four teams in each division. The team that wins the most games in their *geographical division* will compete in their conference playoffs. To give all the teams in a division a fair shot, each team plays every other team in their division twice during the regular season—one home game and one away game.

Unexpected things can happen during the playoffs. A team that has faced strong competition may not have as many wins at the end of the regular season as a team competing against a weaker lineup.

In 2010, the Seattle Seahawks topped their NFC West division with 7 wins to 9 losses— unimpressive, but still the best in the division. Then, in the week after earning a playoff slot, the Seahawks defeated defending Super Bowl champion New Orleans Saints and became the first playoff team with a losing record to win in the post season.

No matter how they get there, once the regular season ends, the four divisional winners are placed in order—1, 2, 3, 4— according to the most wins. These positions are called seeds. In each conference, the number one seed gets a week off (a bye week), while the other winning teams kick off the playoffs against other division winners in their conference.

NFL PLAOFF BRACKET

Here's a question for you. If two teams are sitting out the first weekend of conference playoffs, then who's competing? This is where it gets wild!

Walk on the Wild Side

Speaking of kicking and screaming.... Scruffy, determined, hanging on by a thread, some teams just won't give up. They get banged up and knocked around all season. And still they persist.

They're relentless. These are the six luckiest teams in the NFL—the wild card teams of the season.

Although they didn't win their division, these teams won more games than other *losing* teams in their conference. So, in each conference, AFC and NFC, three teams get to keep playing at least one more week. As a wild card team, they step into seeds 5, 6 and 7 to compete in the playoffs against seeds 2, 3 and 4.

If math isn't your thing, let's break it down:

4 division winners x 2 conferences = 8 teams

3 wild card winners x 2 conferences = 6 teams

8 + 6 = 14 teams that qualify for conference playoffs

Who plays who and when? The two #1 top seeds get a week off. Bye, bye. That "bye" week allows them to rest up while the other teams slug it out. The wild card team with the fewest wins is seed #7. That team plays the second toughest team in their conference, seed #2. The seed #6 wild card team plays seed #3, and seed #5 plays seed #4. The idea, of course, is to give the advantage to the divisional winners by playing top against bottom. Whichever teams win those games will play the following week when seed #1 gets back into the mix.

Why do I want you to care so much about the wild card games? It's not just because playoffs are fun and exciting. They are. It's because wild card teams represent the best in each of us. Sure they're scruffy. But their determination to win can be contagious. And following underdogs can be rewarding, especially if you feel as if you're an underdog in your own life. Watching the wild card games is a way to remind yourself that anything can happen—that you can achieve your dreams and reach your goals.

Of course, this is where the Kick Principle comes in. Wild card players have to dig deep, kick their efforts up a notch or two (or ten), and give it all they've got. I invite you to become a wild card team player. Walk on the wild side and do what no one expects you to do. Do what even *you* don't expect you to do. Surprise yourself. Stand up and show up. Don't focus on the foot of fear, or any obstacle blocking your path. Kick forward in the direction of what you want.

When wild card mentality rules, it means you get to keep competing—in football and in life! And when you think about it, isn't that what really matters?

The Super Bowl

Stars, stats and stash. Two weeks after the playoffs, the winners of the AFC and NFC playoffs go head-to-head in the Super Bowl. These two teams are so hungry for the prize they can taste it. At this point in the season, some players have become mega-stars, securing a place in NFL history and possibly the Pro Football Hall of Fame. Some have charted winning statistics and broken NFL records. And some have signed lucrative contracts simply by getting as far as the "big" game.

Ahhh, the Super Bowl...

- Where the cost to run a 30-second ad in 2021 was about $5.6 million.
- Where over 102 million people from around the world watched the game in 2020.
- Where the price tag to broadcast the season and big game comes to about $3 billion.
- Where *each* player (in 2021) makes $130,000 for winning the Super Bowl.
- Where each player on the losing team gets half of that—$65,000. Each.
- Where over $325 million dollars changes hands just through betting.
- Where huge is spelled e-n-o-r-m-o-u-s.

Yes, the Super Bowl is all that, and its popularity continues to grow. Three networks—CBS, NBC, and FOX—pay a pretty penny to broadcast NFL games throughout the season. They rotate who gets to televise the Super Bowl, so each network gets it once every three years.

Super Bowl commercials have a life of their own. Every year, the bar keeps rising on everything from cinematography and special effects to humor and storytelling. There's even a website dedicated to Super Bowl Ads which includes the latest news and an archive of ads over the years. One 2020 ad by Secret sold a filled football stadium on how magnificent it was that a winning kick was made by a woman. As they were selling their female deodorant products, they were also selling the concept of "Let's Kick Inequality." Smart.

And last but not least, there's the ring. The Super Bowl ring is a coveted symbol of victory, excellence and grit in the NFL. Each year, the NFL gifts 150 rings to the winning team for their coaches, trainers, staff, executives, personnel and, of course, players—whether or not they actually played in the game. And if they imagined themselves playing in it? Well, that counts, too.

Mind Over (Gray) Matter

Purpose. Passion. Pictures. In the previous chapter, I recalled the old joke, Q. "How do I get to Carnegie Hall?" A: *"Practice, practice, practice!"* As a musician, I smile because I know how essential it is to commit to a practice regime. But I also know it's not everything. That's like saying all it takes for a defensive lineman to play in the Super Bowl is to deadlift 600 pounds, or bench 400. Your purpose and passion get you into the weight room or out onto the playing field. They place you in the "red zone" of your goal.

Kicking yourself across the goal line takes something more. It takes pictures. It takes visualizing what and who surrounds you after your future success, as in that vision room I described earlier. Where does your movie making take place? It turns out you have a personal multiplex cinema projector inside your brain, primarily in the prefrontal cortex. This is where your brain learns, remembers, and makes sense of thoughts and actions. It's where you focus your attention and conform everything you do to your internal goals.

Mental visualizations are powerful. If you mentally review specific scenarios, then when you physically enter that situation, your brain is already familiar with possible outcomes, or at least desired ones. That mental rehearsal guides you to make choices and take actions, even physical actions, that support your vision. George Kittle, San Francisco 49ers tight end, says, "I visualize myself making this play on 4th down, so when the game finally comes and [my] number is called, I've already made the play."

Consider Michael Phelps, winner of 28 Olympic medals. While his physical ability is unquestioned, it was his mental game that kept putting him in the Super Bowl of his sport. Phelps envisioned himself winning in a variety of circumstances. He pictured himself sitting in the bleachers with the crowd as he mentally watched himself break another world record. Or he'd see himself at the other end of the pool, watching as he touched the wall to achieve a win.

Phelps visualized absolutely every scenario he could think of that might occur during a swim meet. And then he visualized what he would do if it actually happened. For example, what if his goggles broke? By imagining how he would resolve this issue, Phelps created an *if-then* scenario in his brain. And *if* his goggles *should* break during a competition, his brain would recognize the familiar scenario and go right to work on the solution Phelps had envisioned.

New Orleans Saints' quarterback and Super Bowl MVP Drew Brees says it this way, "My body can only go as far as my mind can take it." Let your mind take you where you want to go.

Visualizing an outcome in your own life might be just the internal kick you need to push across your own goal line. And you can have fun doing it. Think about it—you get to make stuff up and spend time in your happy vision room—and it's free! So, don't hold back. Go for it. Make your vision, or your vision room, as grand as you can possibly imagine it. As Walt Disney said, "If you can dream it, you can do it."

Building Belief

Crafting a virtual reality can be fun, but it can also pose a challenge. After all, it's a lot easier to change the destination of your road trip than it is to pull off the highway of life and re-envision a "future" you. One reason is that you're often pulling the weight of your past along with you, a past packed tightly in a mental U-Haul trailer you can't ditch no matter how hard you try. The beauty of visualizing is that it allows you to break from reality and unhook that trailer of limiting beliefs—at least for a few minutes at a time.

Another challenge to visualizing is the "prove it to me" position. That's when you say, "I'll believe it when I see it," and then wait for your dream to materialize before allowing yourself to believe it can happen. Try flipping it around and do what Michael Phelps, Drew Brees and George Kittle did—envision a clear image of what you want to achieve first. Your brain can be an amazing servant, but *you* have to be the master if you want it to serve you. You have to teach your brain to "see" what you want first, before you can expect yourself to believe it will happen. Seeing it mentally will build your belief.

Wait—what? You can build belief? Don't you just believe in something or not? Though I'm encouraging you to flip the order of things—vision first, then belief—beliefs themselves don't have on/off switches. They are cultivated and strengthened over time through conditioning and repetition. Who's doing the cultivating? That's where it gets complicated.

Babies begin life with a blank slate. They're not born *with* beliefs—they're born *into* them. Their beliefs develop from parental influence and through cultural, geographical, and environmental norms. A child raised in New York City will not grow up with the beliefs and expectations of a youngster in a remote Nepalese village.

Fast forward to adulthood and there's good news—*you're* in charge! You get to choose your beliefs, cultivate and even enlarge them. Bruce H. Lipton, PhD, renowned cell biologist and author of the book *Biology of Belief: Unleashing the Power of Consciousness, Matter and Miracles*, says belief is a biological reaction. According to Lipton, "Genes are not self-actualizing. Meaning they are not capable of controlling their own activity"... meaning, says me, your motor nerve cells can be influenced by your thoughts.

When Michael Phelps mentally envisioned his "if–then" scenarios, he was training more than his brain. He was training his cells to react more quickly to a very specific set of circumstances. By visualizing himself achieving his desired outcome, Phelps was building his belief that he *could* win, even if his goggles broke.

Remembering and replaying a winning feeling is another way to build belief. If you were "in the zone" and achieved success at something in the past, associating that memory with a current goal reminds your brain how success feels. You were successful before, so why not again? I still replay my mental movies of playing tackle football on a grassy field. They remind me I'm strong and brave—and how it feels to be in flow with my intent.

As Oprah Winfrey says, "You don't become what you want, you become what you believe." Yet there's even more packed into the power of building belief. When you believe something is going to happen, when you're absolutely certain of it, something inside you shifts, and you begin to *expect* it to happen. Desire, belief, then expectation. So, "Roll camera!" and direct a mental movie of what you want. Then replay the movie to build your belief and watch as your expectation of having it kicks in.

Kick it Up a Notch

Now that you've got a mental movie of what you want, let's consider how you play it. Do you run it on a big 4K screen in your mind or a small-screen mobile device? How often do you watch it? Is it a fleeting thought you have once a week? Or do you review it several times a day with intent, adding more detail each time?

In other words, does your movie stand out over all the other movies playing in your brain? Is it getting the attention it deserves and needs to actually create change?

A human brain has about 86 billion neurons. Each neuron fires at a rate of approximately 200 times per second and connects to 1,000 other neurons at each firing. When I did the math, my calculator showed 1.72e16, which is 172 quadrillion neuron firings. Per second.

Let's bring the numbers down to earth. In a Newsweek article, Jason Murdock sites a staggering statistic from a team of psychology experts at the Queen's University in Canada. Their research found that humans typically have 6,200 thoughts a day. To get your brain's attention, and make sure your mental movie stands out, you have to kick it up a notch. Supersize it, if you will.

You can visualize an outcome by a variety of methods. I enjoy teaching dynamic visualization. In this approach, you visualize success, or "if-then" scenarios, in a dynamic way—making the images or movies in your mind grand, remarkable, outrageous, even funny. You give characters personality and activate your senses by adding a music track, smells and bright colors. Giving your mental movies extra punch in this way strengthens the neural pathway connections so you reflexively make a choice in life that puts you closer to some aspect of your movie.

When you put your amazing focusing machine into action, it's a little like working out without leaving your chair. A recent article by Janette Hynes and Zach Turner, "Positive Visualization and Its Effects on Strength Training," states, "Just as performing a movement develops muscle memory, actively visualizing a movement can also improve muscle efficiency during a task."

This isn't new information to athletes. According to John Reid of The Florida Times Union, Jacksonville Jaguars kicker Josh Lambo, who has a field-goal success rate of 88.9%, visualizes his kick and kickoffs before they happen. "On Saturday mornings, our specialist's group goes out and we have a full visualization session," says Josh. "I will work on my kickoff steps, visualize everything with no football." Lambo adds, "I think visualization is an important thing, it allows you to save your reps."

The real test is this. If all your thoughts were laid out on a daily chart, would your mental movie be more than a blip in your day? Would your vision movie rise above the competing 6,199 other thoughts you're likely to have in a day? You may have to dig deep to make your movie shine on the big screen in your mind. But that's what the Kick Principle is about—pushing yourself to do that one little seemingly impossible thing that will make a huge difference in achieving your goal.

A League of Their Own

I had a goal: to play tackle football. When I saw the notice to try out for the newly formed Los Angeles Lasers professional women's football team in the summer of 2001, I didn't hesitate for a second. I loved football so much, I wanted to be *inside* the sport, not watching from the sidelines. So, I dug deep, went to tryouts and pushed myself out on that field. (Kudos to WPFL, the Women's Professional Football League for giving me that opportunity.) As the first women's tackle football league, the WPFL was active from 1999 to 2007 and comprised teams across the country—including my LA Lasers.

The idea of women playing tackle football is not, however, as new as you may think. In 1926, an NFL team called the Frankford Yellow Jackets (predecessors of the Philadelphia Eagles) used a women's football team for halftime entertainment. In 1939, a Los Angeles women's softball team, the Marshall-Clampett Amazons, played football during the softball off season to entertain during the Great Depression. The WPFL can be traced back to 1966, when it was first created as a semi-pro league to be a gimmick.

Fast forward 50+ years—and women weren't playing merely for someone else's entertainment. In 2009, the Women's Football Alliance (WFA) began its inaugural season with a whopping 36 teams. Some of those teams came from other leagues, such as the WPFL, the National Women's Football Association (NWFA), and the Independent Women's Football League (IWFL).

In 2018, a new league was forged—the Women's National Football Conference. Through the passion and vision of CEO and Co-Founder Odessa Jenkins, the WNFC has formed 22 teams with 1,000 women and coaches in 18 states. Odessa has attracted major financial sponsors, including Adidas and Riddell, and believes, as I profess in this book, that sports is a microcosm of life. "It can create possibilities in our brains that we can be something that maybe we couldn't see before." Odessa talks about young girls using the experience to break through mental barriers. To change their thinking to: "Maybe if I can be a linebacker, then I can be president."

Women's tackle football is not just an American sport. In 2010, the IFAF—International Federation of American Football—brought together women's tackle football teams from several countries to compete in Stockholm, Sweden. Three years later, the federation hosted the second Women's World Championship in Vantaa, Finland. And in 2017, the third event was held in Langley, Canada. Countries represented were the U.S., Great Britain, Canada, Finland, Australia, and Mexico.

As of 2020, the Women's Football Alliance (WFA) had expanded to include international teams as part of their league. Says Lisa King, WFA Commissioner, "We are proud of how far we have come in a short time and impressed with the level of football being played on the field, but we are even more excited about the promising future that exists for all our players and teams."

If you want to see the WFA in action, watch this video promo for the 2021 season. And if you want to watch a live online WNFC game, here's their schedule.

Women in the NFL

Determination. Focus. Time. A league of their own. And finally... "C-R-A-C-K." There goes the NFL glass ceiling. Did it start with the first female sideline reporters, whose passion for the game was undeniable? Or maybe it was the women's football leagues. Today, women are occupying more major roles in the NFL than ever before.

As of this writing, eight women have coaching positions, while many others have supporting roles. Four women own NFL teams, and five women are NFL officials—one officiated the 2021 Super Bowl. With a fan base of almost 50% women, it's about time women take their place *inside* the game.

One woman has started a tectonic shift by pushing the limits from the inside. Since 2016, Samantha Rapoport, NFL's Senior Director of Diversity, Equity and Inclusion, has been creating opportunities for women to prosper in what has been a male-dominated sport. "I've always been in love with the sport and still am," says Rapoport. "I just knew that it's what I was put on this planet to do. I was put here to help make the game better and stronger." Rapoport's strong kick on the NFL glass ceiling put an "open" sign for women on the NFL's front door.

Case in point—the Tampa Bay Buccaneers won the 2021 Super Bowl with the help of two kick-ass female assistant coaches, Lori Locust and Maral Javadifar. "The female thing? That door needs to be broken down," said Tampa Bay's head coach Bruce Arians before the 2021 Super Bowl. "There are so many good female coaches out there. A player wants to know, 'Can you make me better?' They don't care what color your skin is, what your gender is. If you can make me better, I'm listening."

If you watched the 2020 Super Bowl, you were introduced to Katie Sowers, who was an offensive assistant coach for the San Francisco 49ers. The Microsoft commercial showed footage of her as a child expressing her desire to play football. Even at that age, she seemed to be running a mental movie of herself inside the game. Since the 49ers played in the Super Bowl, that made Katie the first woman to ever coach in the Super Bowl. And Katie is openly gay. So—CRACK + CRACK!

During Super Bowl 2020 media week, Katie told NBC Sports, "Look at me now. Look at us now. All these . . . coaches, they've been doubted in their lives. They've faced adversity. We all have. All you can do is just continue to grind, continue to work, and show everybody what you're capable of." I'd say that's a very good motto for anyone practicing the LIPSTICK Football "Kick" principle.

In addition to female trainers and support staff on NFL teams, there are female officials maintaining the rules of the game. In 2019, Sarah Thomas became the first female on-field official to call an NFL playoff game. And in 2021, Sarah became the first woman to officiate at a Super Bowl game. To reach this position, Sarah probably achieved more "firsts" than any male in her position. She was the first woman to officiate a major college football game, a college bowl game, and a Big Ten Conference game.

In 2021, Sarah was joined by Maia Chaka, the first black woman named to the NFL officiating staff. "I am honored to be selected as an NFL official," said Maia through the NFL. "But this moment is bigger than a personal accomplishment. It is an accomplishment for all women, my community, and my culture." Another double crack in the ceiling.

NFL executive vice president of football operations, Tony Vincent, sees it the same way. "Maia is a trailblazer as the first Black female official and inspires us toward normalizing women on the football field." I like the sound of that. Bring it on!

Do women own NFL teams? As of this writing, there are four NFL female team owners who came to their position through family ties, which doesn't mean they are any less passionate than their male counterparts about their teams or their roles as team leaders. Interested in their story? NFL Films produced a documentary for its 100th anniversary season in 2019 featuring the Fab Four called "A Lifetime of Sundays."

What about football operations? Any women running the show? In May, 2021, Kelly Kleine was hired to be executive director of football operations and special adviser to the general manager of the Denver Broncos. Says Kelly, "You don't have to play football to work in the NFL." Kelly will have significant scouting responsibilities and oversee several football departments. Here's a peek at other influential women in the NFL.

With more and more women entering the game and creating "firsts," you might ask yourself, "Are we in the middle of a LIPSTICK Football revolution?" Sam Rapoport says, "If there are people here who don't believe in women in football, I sure have not come across them." She's not alone in wanting to "normalize women in football." Most women involved with the game would like to see it evolve to the point where earning a staff or team position wouldn't necessarily be considered a "first"—but simply "the next."

Play Like a Girl

If the NFL glass ceiling is cracking, it's partly because they need to make way for the trailblazing young women in colleges and high schools across America who love football and are inserting themselves into the game.

In the 2020 NCAA football season, Vanderbilt coach Derek Mason was hampered by Covid restrictions and player availability for a major conference game. He turned to Sarah Fuller, who was the goalkeeper for the Vanderbilt women's soccer team. Sarah stepped in and, in her second game, kicked for an extra point—making her the first woman to score in an NCAA Division I conference game.

Notice the back of her helmet: "Play Like a Girl."

A tweet by Sarah's soccer team said it all:

"Glass. Everywhere."

Vanderbilt Soccer ✓ @VandySoccer · Nov 28, 2020
Glass. Everywhere.

#AnchorDown

Sarah wasn't the first woman to play college football. There were others who paved the way. In 1997, Liz Heaston was the first woman to score in a college game, followed by Ashley Martin in 2001. Katie Hnida, in 2003, became the third woman to score in a regular season NCAA Division I game. In 2019, Toni Harris became the first woman to receive a four-year football scholarship as a non-specialist—by playing defensive back. Toni was featured in a 2019 Super Bowl ad.

Toni Harris takes playing football seriously, and she isn't shy about sharing her goal: "I want to be the first NFL female player. It's my dream and I'm going to protect it at any cost." Harris clearly lives by the LIPSTICK Football principles and, clearly, she grasps how to approach the game. "It's 80% mental and only 20% physical, so you have to have a different mentality to play the game of football." Harris is also a gracious role model. "I'm just paving the way for the next little girl who is going to come along and be a role model as well."

While you won't find any strictly female high school tackle football teams in America, at least not yet, thanks to Title IX (of the Education Amendments Act of 1972), if a girl wants to play, she can try out. And many have—fair is fair. In Ocean Springs, Mississippi in 2018, Kaylee Foster, after being crowned homecoming queen, won the game by kicking a winning extra point in overtime. Also, in 2018, placekicker Mika Makekau set the state record for the longest field goal (44 yards) by a female kicker.

The future looks bright for girls wanting to play high-school football. A whopping 2,404 girls played on boys' teams in the 2018-2019 school year, more than any other year. And there's a ton of support being offered by sports companies and NFL teams to continue that trend.

Just prior to the 2021 Super Bowl, Nike announced a partnership with the NFL for a $5 million multi-year initiative to develop Girls Flag Football in high school. The Tampa Bay Buccaneers recently allocated $250,000 to creating the first ever Girls Flag Football scholarship program. And several states, such as Georgia, Florida and Nevada, have started to sanction Girls Flag Football as an official high-school sport.

Is there a rung on the ladder for younger girls who love football? Pop Warner, with 250,000 registered players ages five to fourteen, says about one percent are girls. When that representation is spread out to include all youth football programs, it shows an estimated 25,000 girls are playing tackle football.

I'm thrilled for this new progress. On a personal note, I'd like to add—tackle football rocks! I believe tackle football strengthens women—from the outside in, and then back out again. When women learn to stand strong against the defensive forces in their lives, they become unstoppable forces of good in *all* of our lives.

But whether tackle or touch, as Assistant Coach Sowers says, "I am a strong believer that the more we can expose children to a variety of different opportunities in life, the better chance they have of finding their true calling."

Kicks make cracks.

Huddle Up

This chapter has documented many of the firsts that mark the history of women in football. Bear in mind one important feature of the way these women became firsts. In all their lives, self-defeat was the *last* thing they would have done. To become firsts, these women had to hold on to their vision and keep their dream alive. They had to sharpen their focus and visualize their kick-ass win.

Kick-ass on and off the field is powerful. Anytime *you* do something kick-ass, it has a ripple effect. It touches others, whether you know them or not. That Super Bowl ad about Katie Sowers as a child knowing she wanted to be involved with football? Imagine the young girls who were empowered by seeing that. So, never underestimate the power of your own actions. As Katie says, "Show everybody what you're capable of."

And if you appreciate art as life, here's an illustration of the choreography of a thought moving through your brain—an artful representation by Mikael Haggstrom, based on images by Andrew Gillies and Patrick J. Lynch. Maybe this will inspire you to activate your neurons and create a strong, dynamic picture of yourself winning by rising above the fray.

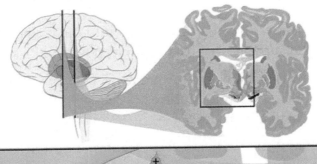

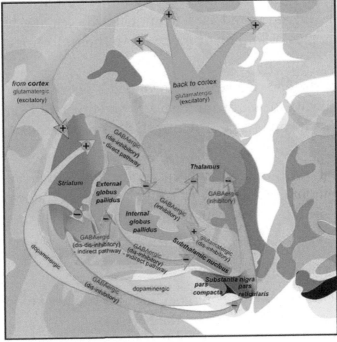

Break It Down

What drives you forward? Is it part of the desire or dream you cultivated in chapter 4? A feeling of accomplishment when you initiated action in chapter 7? Or an image from your vision room? By aligning with those desires and feelings, you can build belief and expect kick-ass results from your actions.

FOOTBALL

1. As you watch a football game, key into the kicker. Watch the gentle run-up followed by a decisive, powerful kick.

2. Watch when a team is in the red zone—the 20 yards before the end zone. Do you notice a change of energy? More determination, perhaps?

3. Record and study the last five minutes of a game. Watch how players dig deep and kick it up a notch—leaping higher to catch a pass or leaping over players (or both) to cross the goal line.

4. Before the end of a season, download a playoff template and fill it in with the four winning teams and three wild-card teams from each conference. Then track their progress to the Super Bowl.

5. Pick at least one woman in football to watch and track throughout the season. That could be a coach, trainer, official, team owner, or even announcer. Share her success with a friend.

LIFE

1. How close are you to your goal line? Do you need to identify a red zone where you turn on the heat?

2. How can you kick your efforts into high gear? Allot more time? Clarify your focus? It's okay to reach out and build a special teams unit to help.

3. Do you have the heart of a wild-card team? Do you stay focused on your wins even when your losses outnumber them? Do a quick count of your wins—big and small. Recalling them will empower you.

4. If you're new to visualization, here are a few guidelines.

- Sit quietly. Raise the focus of your eyes upward about 20 degrees above the horizon. This triggers REM, rapid eye movement, and slows your brain waves. Close your eyes but hold your eye position. Take deep breaths.

- Your brain can't tell time. When you imagine yourself completing a goal at some point in the future, visualize a present-tense vibe, so your brain believes it's happening now.

- Don't put your thought in negative terms such as "I don't want to lose the Super Bowl." Your brain only hears "I want to lose the Super Bowl." Here is a scientific study about why this happens.

- Like conditioning, playing your movie once in a while won't get your brain's attention. Replay it often to build belief and expectation.

Chapter 10

LEARNING TO WIN

The Fifth Quarter

Champions keep playing until they get it right.

—Billie Jean King, Iconic Tennis Legend

When I played professional women's football (insert final smile emoji here), I had a coach who introduced a new concept to me—the fifth quarter. If you've made it this far, you either love learning about life or love learning about football, and you know there are only four quarters in a football game. The concept of the fifth quarter is all about how you will play or perform in the final stretch towards winning.

When you condition yourself to play a fifth quarter, to go beyond what might be expected, you can stand strong in the fourth and say to any opponent in life, "Is that all you've got?" The fifth quarter concept is like conditioning yourself to run five miles when the race you entered is only three. It's Michael Phelps mentally rehearsing how to fix his broken goggles—*before* they break. It's you—staying out front and on top of your mental game so you can clear a path, take the ball and run.

To stay in front of your pursuit, as I mentioned in chapter 1, you need guiding principles like the eight I have tested and shared with you. I hope the LIPSTICK Football principles help you, as they have me, to place a worthwhile dream at the finish line and reach it with breath to spare.

I presented these principles in a specific order to provide structure to your thinking. They also encourage you to reflect on your choices: when have you been as conscious as the situation demanded, when . . . not so much? There's a term for this—it's *metacognition*, which is simply the awareness and understanding of one's own thought process.

I incorporate the LIPSTICK Football principles in my own thought process. When I'm at an impasse or blocked by a challenge, I mentally run down the list of eight principles. Invariably, one pops out and *speaks* to me, guides me—to take a leap, immerse myself, track my actions, or kick my efforts up a notch. Now that you've learned the principles, you can use *your* metacognition—your awareness and understanding—to identify the principle you might need at any given time.

Do you have a champion's heart? Before you answer, key into the first part of Billie Jean King's quote, "Champions keep playing..." Champions are fifth-quarter players, fifth-quarter students of life. They show up and keep learning, working, trying, learning, working, trying...believing. And they love playing the game. It's not always easy, but champions endure. As author Angela Duckworth says, "Enthusiasm is common. Endurance is rare." If you want to live life like a champion, keep showing up and keep playing.

This chapter will wrap up with a few extra tips to help you shine through your fifth quarter. And the *LIPSTICK Football* principles, in whatever order you use them, will provide steady guidance as you make forward progress toward your destination. Together, they will help you become the champion you were meant to be.

Zigzag Your River of Dreams

Billy Joel wrote a song called "The River of Dreams." In it, he talks about losing something meaningful, something sacred, and needing to cross a wide river to find it.

I like to use Billy Joel's lyric as a metaphor for goal setting in life. The river represents the great divide between where you are and where you want to be, or who you want to become. Where "the river is wide," your goals and aspirations seem impossible to reach. They might as well be at the far end of eternity. In chapter 7, I introduced distal (long-term) goals and proximal (short-term) goals. Do you recall which has the higher success rate? Yep, short-term goals. When you set a goal so close you can *almost* reach it, you're likely to stretch yourself to do just that.

My neighborhood has a few hills. I live on top of one. When I go for a bike ride, I fly down the hill then ride around in the flatter section. Coming back home? No way I could bike straight up the hill—it's a doozy. It's like trying to reach the end zone on a football field in a single play. So I break down my ascent into segments—zigzagging at a 45-degree angle from one side to the other. On some days, I have to adjust to a 30-degree angle. That's okay. The point is, with each zig and zag, I achieve my goal and get to the top of that damned hill.

Let's apply this zigzagging to your "river of dreams." You may want with all your heart to throw an inner tube, kayak or canoe into the river and just go for it. But if you head straight down the middle, from point A to point Z, you'll get toppled, turned upside down and caught in life's undertow. Instead of rushing toward point Z, divide your journey downstream into small proximal goals. Make them as small as they need to be for you to not only accomplish each goal but to also enjoy getting there.

Call me crazy, but that's a kick-ass approach to life—and any sport you can think of. It's why I love watching football so much. Think about it. Every yard is a win because it gains precious territory on the field. Every 10 yards gets rewarded with a first down, an even bigger win. Until finally you're in the red zone, and then over the goal line. It's never about making it to the end zone, your Point Z destination, in one giant leap. It's about taking individual leaps that propel you forward, one yard at a time, until you're where you want to be.

Embrace Point G

Move toward any long-distance goal and you'll come to a place I like to call "Point G." Whether you arrive at Point G by chance or intent, getting there means you're about a third of the way toward your end goal, Point Z. Yay! Give yourself a pat on the back. You've reached a milestone and completed a substantial chunk of your goal. While you're still in progress moving down your river of dreams, stopping at Point G is a way of acknowledging your commitment to staying on course and advancing toward your goal surely and steadily.

What's cool about Point G is that it's closer to being a proximal goal than a distal goal, and proximal goals are easier to achieve. If you have the football on your 20-yard line, it's a heck of a lot easier to focus on getting to the 50-yard line than all the way downfield to the end zone. Getting to Point G will take more effort to reach than, say, Point B or C—and you might have to stretch to get there—but focusing on getting to Point G can build confidence and reduce stress. Once you reach it, you will have tasted success with gathering momentum in the desired direction. You will feel motivated to build momentum again, and this time you start from a point closer to your ultimate goal.

Another benefit of stopping at Point G is that when you're closer to your distal goal, that big-picture dream, you gain a different perspective. When you stand on the 50-yard line of a football field, you have a clearer view of the end zone than if you were on the 20-yard line. Seeing your destination more clearly helps you make better choices about how to get there—or determine if "there" is still where you want to go. By using Point G as a plateau or rest stop for reflection, you can track your progress and fine-tune your plan, then realign yourself so your efforts are efficient and effective.

What's the point I'm making? Embrace Point G. Look for it. Anticipate it. That's you at the helm of the craft moving down river toward your dreams. Recall the benefit of a football time-out. You get to decide when to pull over to the river's edge and reset your course, or simply acknowledge how far you've come. If you need a reminder to look for Point G, there are some good "G" words that can help you. Good. Glad. Grateful. Goal-oriented. Groovy. Glorious. And of course—Go Get 'Em!

A lot can change on a journey. I've upended a few different road trips because I saw a road sign or took an exit that led me to a different destination, something closer to my heart. I'm not encouraging you to change course a lot as you move towards your goal or destination. Keep a steady course, but do listen to your heart and, whether for a minute or a month, pause to take in the glorious view from Point G.

Win or Learn—You Can't Get It Wrong

I would not be a good coach or motivational author if I didn't quote Yoda. So here you go, *"The greatest teacher, failure is."* Trying new things or finding new ways of doing something isn't always easy. And when the stakes are high and the outcome is important, you may hesitate from taking action altogether. Why? Do you fear you might get it wrong? Does that feel like failing? Unfortunately, humans are good at keeping score of their failings and keeping their memories of failing alive.

If you never had to worry about getting something wrong, would you be more adventurous? Would you try something new? Would you push yourself a little farther toward your goal? As a baby learns to walk, any forward progress is considered a success by her doting parents, no matter how wobbly the effort. Even falling down is a win, because she strengthens her little legs as she steadies herself to stand up again. And again and again.

If you need a more secure footing for your wobbly legs, let me offer you a gift—it's a sort of "Get out of Jail Free" card. It reads, "You can't get it wrong." I got this card from the American inventor Thomas Edison. Let me explain.

In 1879-1880, Edison invented the incandescent light bulb. It took 10,000 tries to create a light bulb that worked. When someone suggested he'd failed 10,000 times, Edison said, "I didn't fail 10,000 times. I learned 10,000 ways it didn't work." To Edison, those 10,000 tries weren't mistakes. Each effort gave him valuable knowledge he used to improve and finesse his process until he found a workable solution. He tested and observed, made improvements from his observations, retested, improved more— and repeated the process—10,000 times.

Approaching life from a perspective of learning is what champions do, and Edison is an all-star champion. According to The Franklin Institute, Edison said, "The electric light has caused me the greatest amount of study and has required the most elaborate experiments." He added, "I was never myself discouraged, or inclined to be hopeless of success. I cannot say the same for all my associates."

While you may think the light bulb is one of Edison's great achievements, personally I think not being "hopeless of success" during 10,000 attempts is worth shouting about. It reminds me of football games when the losing team is down too much to recover. Yet the quarterback stands strong and the team plays as though it really *could* win.

No matter how bad you feel you're doing at something, remember—that's a feeling, not a fact. It's a perspective, and a temporary one at that. Read the Edison quote again. From his perspective, creating the light bulb caused "the greatest amount of study." He treated his experiment as a puzzle he was trying to solve. He added "[it] required the most elaborate experiments." There's nothing in his remark that hints of "getting it wrong." Just tracking, learning and applying what he learned, until he got it *right*. In fact, it sounds as if he was having a good time learning what *not* to do.

Will reaching for what you want take, in Edison's words, your "greatest amount of study?" Maybe. Throughout every football season, teams are constantly adjusting their plays and players based on what they learn game-to-game. The key is—don't get angry at your mistakes. Welcome them. And keep in mind the second half of Billie Jean King's quote, "Champions keep playing...*until they get it right.*" If you're a champion, you'll keep playing *and* learning—and commit to as many tries as it takes to get it right.

Ready to Win?

As Head Coach of the LIPSTICK Football League, let me leave you with this this final thought. Whether your goal is to play sports, write a book, or invent a light bulb—you will run into challenges. But the human spirit is resilient and strong. I believe you can always find a resolution through process.

If you find yourself struggling, consider choosing a different goal, one that's a better fit for you. You have so many special attributes that make you the unique individual you are. Keep an eye open for what you absolutely love doing. Know when you shine and when you may need to reposition yourself to project your inner light.

Remember, a football team reveals its strengths not in a single play but in how the players approach getting the ball downfield. That process of evaluation, adjustment and action isn't performed just once but many times throughout the game and season. And while the goal line is an important marker, the quality of the process is what generates momentum and forward progress—in football and in life.

The eight LIPSTICK Football principles add up to a powerful process. By supporting your process and learning from it, you're going to win. You're going to win big. Because the biggest win in life isn't about winning the game each and every time— it's about learning *how* to win. It's about taking control of your journey. Finding balance and joy in your choices. Making choices that encourage growth and expand your possibilities.

Are you ready to win? Are you ready to start using the LIPSTICK Football method and step into a lifelong competition with yourself for your personal best? You have nothing to lose— and everything to gain. So, suit up! It's time to start winning— The LIPSTICK Football way.

Thank You!

Thank you for buying my book. If you enjoyed my unique mashup of football and life, please leave a review on the Amazon book page to let others know this book can be valuable for them as well.

To leave a review:

1. Sign into your Amazon account.
2. Go to the book page for LIPSTICK FOOTBALL.
3. Scroll down to the Customer Reviews section.
4. Find "Review this product" and click on the "Write a customer review" button.

Free Gift

Subscribe to the LIPSTICK FOOTBALL League and claim your free "I Love You…But" exercise from my next book, *LIPSTICK FOOTBALL Workbook* (coming Fall 2021).

www.LipstickFootball.com/action

About the Author

Hi there. I'm Diana Weynand, or Coach D. You know by now that I love football and I love to "carpe vita" – seize life – by following a clear set of principles and taking action on them. It's my mission to empower people to mastermind their lives by doing the same thing.

I love writing, coaching, speaking and motivating groups—large and small, young and not as young. I love the challenge of "cracking a marble" and breaking down a complex challenge, goal or project into actionable steps

Given the choice, I'd almost always rather play and throw the ball on a field than watch other people have fun doing it on TV. I shine when I perform music and produce shows. I'm passionate about protecting nature and the environment, and I commit my leadership skills to climate nonprofit organizations. I'm a sailor and I love being out on the water.

However challenging and messy it may be at times; I love my life. As Helen Keller said, "Life is either a daring adventure or nothing at all." I choose adventure.

Other Books

You can find my video and editing books on my Amazon author page. To be notified about new release updates for *LIPSTICK FOOTBALL* and other upcoming books, go to my Amazon author page and click the Follow button.

To reach out with stories or input, contact:

info@LipstickFootball.com

LIPSTICK FOOTBALL Method Workshops, Speaking and Consulting

If you would like to use the LIPSTICK Method
to motivate your company, school, team or organization,
contact us to schedule a workshop or speaking engagement:

info@LipstickFootball.com

Get Into Action!

For access to additional resources mentioned in the book that
will help you take a deeper dive into the LIPSTICK Method,
visit the Lipstick Football Extras page:

www.LipstickFootball.com/extras

Life Coaching

If you are interested in personal life coaching,
please visit my coaching site:

www.MastermindLife.com

Be Generous

If you learned something about life and football,
consider gifting this book to a friend, family member or
colleague. More often than not, watching football *and* living life
are group activities. The more people you can include in your
new LIPSTICK FOOTBALL circle, the more fun you'll have
watching games and practicing the LIPSTICK Football Method.

Made in the USA
Columbia, SC
23 October 2021